Guilt
Unplugged
Waking up from the lie we live

JOHN FLAHERTY

John Flaherty
www.beawarebealive.com

Book design
www.thomgray.co.uk

Cover image
H. Heyerlein

ISBN-13: 978-1978393448
ISBN-10: 197839344X

CONTENTS

The search for truth is a cooperative, unending endeavour.
We should engage in it to the extent we can, seeking
to free ourselves from constraints imposed by coercive
institutions, dogma, irrationality, excessive conformity, lack
of initiative and imagination, and numerous other obstacles.
As for possibilities, they are limited only by will and choice.

Noam Chomsky

THE IMPORTANCE AND VALUE OF THIS BOOK. Humanity has the enormous task of regaining its freedom. We may all THINK we have freedom, but that's only because we've been repeatedly told we have it. In truth, the freedom we believe we possess cannot be compared to the free expression we naturally demonstrated as an infant.

Every child instinctively desires freedom and every particle of their being exudes the magnetic energy of unrestricted joy, unbridled imagination, unlimited possibilities and natural wonder, just as your Life did, before you knew of guilt. The imposition of guilt in a child's psyche, and the feeling of shame which results from that imposition, never needs to be the experience a child encounters. It never needed to be instilled in you, but it was, and you've continued to struggle with the consequences of its entrapment ever since.

To make matters more confusing, the popular thinking in the world is that guilt is both essential and often helpful to our moral functioning, that it is part of our biology, one of our emotions, and synonymous with conscience. Yet, in reality, we cannot possibly experience freedom, while guilt crushes heart, spirit, mind and will.

Throughout the pages of this book it is my intention to open up for you the possibility to enjoy a very different Life experience. When you are resourced to embrace Life from a deeper place of awareness, you will find that no matter what you've been taught to believe, and no matter what you may have ever *done* to make you feel so 'wrong', guilt does not have to be the consequence that keeps you forever in its stranglehold. The importance and value of this book is for you to know and become aware that there is another way to find the freedom you seek. All you need to grant yourself, is your own permission to live it.

THE PROMISE OF THIS BOOK. You have chosen to read this book because your Life has repeatedly experienced restriction and limitation, and, you can be sure that guilt has been the cause of that restriction. Guilt has either made you feel unworthy of Life, not entitled to it, or you have become so conditioned and programmed to conform to the mind-set of guilt, that you've been robbed of your own personal sovereignty; a free heart, spirit, mind and will.

Because you have not been taught to question the many ways humanity has been consistently programmed to accommodate guilt, you will most likely have remained unaware of just how much you are conditioned by it. You will have been unaware that within you has grown some kind of 'duty' or obligation to get Life 'right'. And, contrived as it is, you will have similarly formed in your mind the strange idea that you could possibly get Life 'wrong'!

The promise of this book is your freedom. I realise that may sound like a very bold claim, but I make it with great confidence. Those of you who have read and practised the teaching of *Addiction Unplugged : How To Be Free* will know that by deepening your awareness, your Life has undergone an enormous shift. The message of that Life-giving book has been so readily greeted across the world, that within just two years of its first publication it became available in five different languages. The precious message of the book you now have in your possession will enable you to make the shift you also yearn to experience. Your deepening awareness changes everything, and this book promises to lovingly guide you through that liberating process.

Throughout our existence many of us, perhaps almost all of us, have been made to feel guilty. In most cases, our first encounter with guilt started in our earliest years and, as time has gone on, guilt has become so deeply embedded in our unconscious mind that we now find it difficult to imagine we could ever be free from it. It is also why you've grown to be so resigned to it.

As a child we struggle to make sense of the programming fed to us, which we are expected to conform to and make as our logic. It is a struggle, because it does not necessarily fit with our actual daily experiences of Life at all. But we do try. In fact we try so hard and for so long to justify the programming we've been given, that we begin to feel 'duty-bound' to it. We develop a sense of loyalty to *everything* that was passed on to us and find ourselves defending and justifying all that we've been taught to embody, no matter what inaccuracies, falsehoods or untruths may have been imparted to us. Though much of our programming may never have truly made logical sense to us, we rarely question its validity or how beneficial its function is in our lives. This is how you have remained unconscious of your own personal sovereignty, shallow in your awareness, and so accepting of the idea of guilt, even though its caused you such pain, confusion and conflict.

You could continue to spend the rest of your adult Life justifying your programming, as many people do, and even feeling guilty for the times when you don't quite manage to live up to it! However, I don't recommend that, and, it isn't the reason you bought this book. Also important to understand, is that guilt does not allow healing, recuperation, or peace in those who do not let themselves find the stillness to relax and rest from its disturbing presence. This book will show you *how* to redefine your experience of Life, so you can enjoy every aspect of it, just as you once did before guilt ever became embedded in your psyche. Then you will truly be your Self, living every encounter, every relationship, every new discovery and everything you like in a state of freedom, peace and rest.

THE GIFT OF THIS BOOK. Doing something we know we aren't supposed to isn't where the seeds of guilt are sown and it's terribly important that we get clear about this.

The freedom to truly be ourselves in childhood is something rarely encouraged by adult society, and that is precisely when and why guilt kicks in as we dare to be ourselves anyway. The feeling we internalise as an infant is not primarily a sense that what we are *doing* is wrong, but that *we are* in some way 'wrong' for even wanting to explore a universe that beckons investigation everywhere our gaze falls.

Guilt is first experienced in childhood. It arises as we lose connection with those who demand from us that which we have not yet learned to give. Often it is with those we love most. We want to keep their favour and end any disappointment or dissatisfaction they may have with us but we struggle, simply because we're not yet equipped to share their reasoning or their logic. We cannot always meet the conditions that are set before us. Most parents believe the love and connection they have with their children is unconditional. However, in truth, only a child loves unconditionally. Every adult's Life is pitted with conditions and we all lay down very specific conditions for our children, along with countless demands and expectations of them.

A child must be allowed to be free. If we try to confine the freedom of a child in any way, they will experience the repercussions of our choices. We stifle a child when we constantly correct them in a punishing way, when we belittle them, ignore them, yell at them, or put them down. All of these reactions are destructive and go completely against the Laws of the Universe, because the entire universe is set up to accommodate a child's natural drive to come into 'being'. A child instinctively reaches out to the world it newly finds itself in and with the sole desire to connect, experiment, explore and participate.

The guilt you carry today began when you expressed your own perfectly ordinary desires to extend yourself out into your world. Sadly, it will not always have been met with sufficient acceptance, validation and affirmation from those you most wanted to please. We live in a society that has learned to constrict itself, and there will have been occasions when you have been made to feel 'bad' just for showing up in Life!

Guilt tells you that you cannot do what you want or feel at peace with yourself as you want, because it may be unfair to someone else. The gift of this book is to elicit and restore truth over that lie. When we are free of guilt we can move forward with our lives. We can at last make something of it.

If you remain ignorant of a more conscious way to live your Life, guilt will keep you imprisoned for the rest of your days. And, if you do not discover how to guide a child of yours more consciously, they will also remain burdened by the uselessness of guilt. The gift of this book is to present more conscious options to you, so you may deepen your awareness and make choices which set you free.

My grand nephew, Aidan, now 7 years old, continues to be my own daily inspiration and the provider of much of the wisdom contained in this book, just as he was when I wrote *Addiction Unplugged : How To Be Free*.

Aidan is the constant reminder to me of how more freeing Life is, without the encumbrances of guilt. He has not been introduced to guilt's needless and painful confusion and is not likely to accommodate it as he grows older.

Instead, Aidan has been able to maintain his personal sovereignty as he cultivates his emotional intelligence. Aidan is forming his conscience not from guilt, but from a progressively evolving consciousness. Without guilt, and without ever being made to feel ashamed, he is discovering the value of self and mutual respect. He knows how to always reach for the higher choice and, as a result, Aidan is an impactful presence in the world wherever he goes.

Enjoy this book. Take your time with it. There's much to unravel. Think of Aidan as you read it. And, know that you are really no different from him at all, you'd just forgotten to *remember* your own truth. Then gift yourself freedom. Aidan will remind you how to move through guilt - shame - remorse - regret - and back to connectivity once again.

Getting the most from this book

The real voyage of discovery consists not in seeking new lands but in seeing with new eyes.

–Marcel Proust

Guilt Unplugged is written to set you free. It is to assist you to immediately re-instate truths that are central to your essence and to relieve yourself of the burden of guilt forever. It provides a Life-line to those of you who have struggled, perhaps for a Life-time, with the incessant worry and deep anguish which guilt stirs within us. It equips you with the tools with which to prise yourself free from the wet-suit of guilt's hold and out of despair.

Each chapter contains new insights, new discoveries, new revelations and new truths, raising you to a new level of experience and to a new understanding of Life itself. Essentially, this is a book like no other, for it does not spend time pacifying you or needlessly attempting to make you feel less bad about your feelings of guilt, or of your resulting sense of shame. It does not entertain the notion that a so called 'healthy guilt' is more beneficial than guilt which fosters negative emotions. Guilt's theme song is "I'm damned if I do, and I'm damned if I don't", and it's not a pretty tune. There is no such thing as 'healthy' guilt. If your intention is to be loving, and this includes being loving to yourself, then guilt by any description must not be allowed a place in your Life. This book does not use distinctions between guilt which is thought of as being 'justified' as opposed to guilt which is deemed 'unjustified'. Nothing like that. Rather, the message here is to present revelations that will never have been unveiled to you before, realisations that you have not realised before, and beliefs you have not been taught to question before.

When those revelations are made, when those realisations dawn and as those questions are asked, all you have to do is merely *allow* and be willing to consider differently, the many truths that have remained hidden from you. Once you do that, you will be able to explore the possibility of applying them in your Life and then observing the results. The potential for fulfilment and the sense of completeness each person desires is all around you. You must get out of the box you think you're trapped in and ask yourself: "What will make me feel fulfilled? What will make me feel complete?" Then reach for it.

Know this and become aware ...

As guilt disappears, its associated allies will similarly subside and fall away too; shame, restriction, repression, suppression, depression, addiction.

So that this book can initiate the process of inner transformation and ignite the sense of completeness you desire, the close of each chapter will invite you to pause, reflect and begin to draw in your new found truths about your Self and about Life. Then, the largely un-heard, un-taught, and un-lived message of liberation can be invited by you to take up its new home within you. Though at first your mind may tussle with its new revelation, simply know that that's what the mind does with just about anything that is newly presented to it. The mind always thinks it knows all that there is to know, so don't be too daunted by your mind's little song and dance routine! Just accept that your heart and Soul are already anticipating the Life-giving impact of your new revelations. Your mind will soon be enlightened to follow suit and fall into alignment.

The awakening process to personal freedom is often referred to as enlightenment and, necessarily, is always ongoing and evolutionary. There is no better description of the process of awakening than that so perfectly summed up by the Zen Teacher, Adyashanti. In a few sentences he succinctly puts it this way:

"Make no mistake about it—enlightenment is a destructive process.
It has nothing to do with becoming better or being happier.
Enlightenment is the crumbling away of untruth.
It's seeing through the façade of pretence.
It's the complete eradication of everything we imagined to be true."

Waking up from the *façade* of guilt is no different. Begin your 'waking up' process NOW and, under all circumstances, let the crumbling away of guilt's untruth be thorough, determined and ongoing. Pull down and strip away all falsehoods and all deceptions as you evolve. Then, as new revelations and new realisations become clear to you, it will become possible to move more freely with the flow of Life.

Guilt will only make it feel as if you're always going against the stream. Take heart because the teaching of this book will show you how to remedy that struggle. As you ease into each chapter your knowledge and awareness will be expanded. If some parts of the book seem repetitive, they are there to 're-mind' you about something that I don't want you to forget. Repetition reinforces the circuits in your brain and forms more neural connections so that in your weakest hour, you don't talk yourself out of greatness!

From new revelations new realisations will open up to you. And from those newly unfolding realisations, new found truths will be restored to the centre of your Being. That new-found experience of restoring truth and freedom in place of falsehood and indoctrination is "metanoia".

METANOIA (from the Greek μετάνοια metanoia, changing one's mind, change of heart, a fundamental transformation of core beliefs and limitations through a raising of consciousness.)

We do not really have an English word for metanoia that can adequately convey the meaning of the original Greek word. Although over the centuries Christianity has unsuitably translated metanoia as "repentance", this derivative does not draw from metanoia anything like the depth and richness conveyed by its original Greek meaning. The term "repentance" carries with it a negative tone, more akin to contrition or doing penance for "wrongs" committed. It's the very emphasis of course, which for centuries has had such an overwhelming influence on humanity and which holds such a negatively binding impact on you today, whether you have been aware of its detrimental effects or not.

Even more astonishingly, whether you regard yourself as religious or not, you may be surprised to discover just how much your own psyche has been imprinted by the misinterpretation of this word metanoia and, as a result, by its misplaced influence. For now, simply become aware that guilt has been systematically woven into the collective consciousness of humanity. There is nothing *natural* about guilt and it has nothing to do with what is *wrong* with you. In later chapters, as we delve more deeply into the origins of guilt, you will see how it has kept humanity feeling disconnected from our Source and in ignorance of our true nature. You will also see how insidiously it has been imprinted on our psyche and how its burden has become so instantaneously accepted by each one of us without question.

Unlike Early Christian misinterpretations, the pure meaning of metanoia forces a powerful, pro-active Life-affirming response from those who invite it. Metanoia prompts a shift in our consciousness so we may embody a fundamental change in the trend and action of our whole inner nature. 'Meta' - implies going *beyond* and *outside* of. In the same way the word metaphysics means going beyond the limits of physics, Metanoia is also, a going beyond. It is a leap in consciousness.

Metanoia calls from us a fundamental change in heart, spirit, mind and will, opening up a new future and a more complete way of living. It takes us beyond where the illusionary construct of a dualistic view of Life has taken root and manifested. Metanoia is your entrance into a restored and rejuvenated experience, literally taking your mind/thoughts beyond and *outside of* how you have been thinking, acting, reacting, behaving and engaging in Life, and without any need for guilt. The illusionary construct which guilt is has been keeping us all in servitude to ignorance and, more to the point, has been keeping alive the imaginary chasm between you and the Divine.

If you are ready to embrace the revelation, realisation and transformation of metanoia and feel ready to leave the notion of guilt behind,

Know this and become aware ...

All things are changed once the illusion of ignorance and all your layers of programming have been removed.

REVELATION. True empowerment comes when you start to look deeply at your programmed beliefs and conditioned thoughts and behaviours.

REALISATION. You awaken to a greater reality, opening the way to personal peace and freedom.

METANOIA. The complete unfolding of consciousness, allowing a new understanding of Who You Truly Are. Letting go of the fear-filled, limited being you once believed yourself to be.

Awakening. The Lotus flower symbol illustrates the evolutionary stages of consciousness as you move through guilt and shame to remorse, then from remorse to regret, and from regret to connectivity once again.

CHAPTER ONE

Waking up from the lie we live

After awakening, you no longer derive your sense of who you are from what your mind tells you about you.

–Eckhart Tolle

Guilt is an aspect of consciousness that is residing in us all. Guilt is insidious, destructive, punishing and all-consuming. Guilt turns love into resentment, and then into hatred. It prevents you from experiencing anything that feels good. Guilt tells you that feeling good is wrong. Then it contradicts itself by telling you that you were foolish for not doing what you wanted to do in the first place. Guilt serves only to obliterate from your awareness the natural flow of Life that is constantly supplying each of us. Until you release guilt's falsehood, it will continue to feel completely 'at home' in your Life.

You are now about to reinstate within you the grandeur of your Being, your personal sovereignty, which has become all but lost from the human psyche. The invitation of this book is an invitation to you to raise your consciousness sufficiently, so you may live your Life as it is intended; free from the stranglehold of the unnatural phenomenon which guilt is.

This is a unique book, as you will find. The very fact that it is a book which specifically addresses the phenomenon of guilt is quite unique in itself. For you will now begin to notice, if you had not already noticed before, that not many books are available on the slippery subject of guilt. That is quite remarkable don't you think, given the confusion and suffering guilt brings to each of us?

And ...
Even though guilt is always assumed to be one of our emotions
Even though every single adult person has their own examples of guilt
Even though guilt is so repugnant to everyone
Even though we generally know who or what provokes guilt within us
Even though we are capable of contributing to or evoking guilt in others ...

Everyone remains in obedient acceptance and tolerance of its stranglehold, never thinking to call its bluff and test its truth. So what is this hellish punishing presence that has been given free licence to rule our lives to the extent it does? It is necessary to unearth its hiding places, so you may see its menace in full light.

You may also have noticed that not even the contemporary spiritual teachers of our age, nor the ones who preceded them, have delved very much into the subject of guilt. Those who have written about it, like modern day psychologists and psycho-analysts, have rarely questioned why we are so tolerant of it. We have all just blindly consented to guilt's dominion over us and accepted that it must simply be how we are meant to feel. However, not content to settle for that, this book prompts you to ask yourself;

Why have I become totally spell-bound to believe that I got something so very wrong, and which made me feel so bad, that its indelible stain - that which we call guilt - could last a Lifetime?

Does it not strike you as a little odd, when from every natural wonder created on this earth, you could think yourself to be unworthy of your place in it? Guilt confuses. It makes us all feel displaced and disconnected. Guilt is a burden known to and experienced by every human being and it is so ingrained that we no longer feel compelled to question it. Why? Why is this our experience and why does it not give you an idea of just how much else you have unquestioningly taken for granted?

For example ...
How much more empowered and complete would your Life be without guilt's overbearing harness?

How much easier would it be to live every moment of your Life if you were without guilt's debilitating constraint?

How much more in your Life would you have given yourself the permission to enjoy and be enriched by, had you not felt so duty-bound to accommodate guilt's bizarre party-pooper presence?

How might you be living this very moment if you were without guilt?

How would you be making the very next decision you are just about to make, as you interact with others, choose your friends, choose your partner? How differently would you select your pleasures?

How much more or how much less would you be choosing to instil the familiar punishing experience guilt brings with it, as you automatically impart its uselessness in the hearts and minds of your children?

How, who or what would it take to remove from your Life this disgusting experience named G-U-I-L-T, which we all reluctantly resign ourselves to accept and which lasts with us our whole Life-time?

G-U-I-L-T, so differently interpreted and so uniquely experienced by each individual, still remains the word we all borrow to describe the helplessness and self-loathing which torments us. What the Hell is it? For surely this is no *Heavenly* encounter we experience?

Let's get right to the point, go for the jugular, cut to the chase, enter the realm where even spiritual teachers have rarely gone deep enough. Let's do what every evolving human being must do, in order to be rid of guilt's falsehood. Let's transcend its lie and go beyond its threats once and for all ... Let's discover how to UNREAL it!

The only Life-long antidote to guilt is Self-acceptance. Now Self-acceptance, doesn't just mean learning to feel less bad about yourself, Self-acceptance means fully accepting the fullness of YOU. It is to accept the truth about your very essence and the truth about your essence is that it does not include guilt. So before reading another line of this book or even taking your very next breath, understand this:

You are an Individuation of the Divine.

Now, whatever else you've been taught, no matter what else your thoughts have tortured you over, no matter how big a leap this book may be inviting you to take, just go ahead and draw in a nice deep breath ready for the leap.

No, no, no, that's not a really big deep breath is it? On the other hand, that tiny sip of air you've just meagerly allowed yourself does indicate just how little you believe there is to receive from Life. The small mouthful of air you've just faintly taken in is proportionate to the minuscule entitlement guilt has been allowing you to receive from Life itself! No wonder you've been struggling to live Life in its free flow of natural joy and its total freedom. So go ahead now and defy the lies you've been fed from others about your own true worth or entitlements. Breathe in the total acceptance that you are nothing less than an Individuation of the Divine; the microcosm of the macrocosm of Life itself. Life which knows no lack, no deficiency, no failure, no end, not even death itself. Don't stop off at that death bit, we'll deal with that later ... For now, just go ahead and breathe in, generously.

With each really big intake of breath, deliberately treat yourself to as much of Life as you can. That very act of drawing to yourself all that Life has to offer is indication enough that Life holds no grudge against you. It has no agenda. It does not withhold. It does not judge. It is not out to get you or hold you to account. It is only forever providing, supplying, allowing you to be totally accepting of your own Self. Anyone who may have taught you to believe otherwise, suggested or insisted that you accept some other version of Life, has not yet discovered freedom in their own lives. Nor have they allowed themselves the same permission that you have just granted your Self. Know that there is as much, or indeed as little of Life, as you allow yourself to experience. Draw it in now. That's right, nice and deep. Then exhale. If you enjoyed the new experience, then take in an even bigger one than that. At the same time, receive in your new-found acceptance of your Self.

For Self-acceptance to ultimately emerge and become your new found expression in Life, the past also needs to be put into an entirely new perspective. Not only your past experiences, as you've lived them year in and year out, but the whole of humanity's past in its entirety: how and what you have been taught, the extent to which you have not once questioned the meaning or purpose of Life or your own creative contribution to it, and the judgments you have made about everything.

So that guilt can no longer bind you like a tight wet-suit, it is essential to accept that the whole of humanity has been struggling in auto-pilot mode. Your struggle has been in trying to accommodate an untruth about your very existence. You have been duped into accepting a falsehood about Life, along with a misguided sense of 'duty' to keep the lie of guilt actively present. While you have been allowing guilt to take up space in your own existence, you have also been unwittingly enforcing it in others: partners, loved ones, those you interact with most regularly and, most devastatingly of all, in your children.

We have all been simply re-enacting and regurgitating everything handed down to us from those who have gone before us: parents, teachers, religions, and through our various education systems. Authority figures, who had similarly never paused to question their own origin and true nature or their own personal sovereignty, purpose or responsibilities have each had enormous impact on those they influenced. Those authority figures are not reading this book, but YOU are. Those authority figures never thought to teach the message of this book or pass on to you a version of Life that did not include guilt. You may choose to do differently. Either way, Life is now inviting you to find out for yourself that guilt does not have to be accommodated by you any longer.

No matter what thought, word or deed you feel is so incriminating or so unforgivable about you, know that all is well. No matter how much guilt is telling you right now that you will feel even more guilty if you say "goodbye" to it, just stay calm. Now become aware of your breath. Become aware of your heart. Become aware of your spirit. Take each breath, generously, and know that it's time to take the leap - which may well actually turn out to be not quite as gigantic as you once believed it could be - and read on.

Know this and become aware ...

You can live your Life the hard way or the easy way. You can live Life with guilt or free from it. You certainly weren't born with it, though many of the world's religions have convinced you otherwise.

There was no trace of guilt to inhibit your early formative years. Guilt had to be taught to you and learned by you. It had to be shown to you and re-enforced within you. It had to be indoctrinated and then imprinted. It had to remain unquestioned and therefore remain unmoved. Many things are like that. However, it does not make them acceptable or true. You do not have to make them *real*.

Guilt is not a natural phenomenon, that is why it feels to you like it can neither be satisfied or dissolved. Guilt is always thought of as just one of our emotions, yet it is really an intense underlying *belief* which we hold and carry about ourselves. It is a belief so ingrained that it persistently affects, impacts and influences every other emotion we feel. We can experience the heaviness of guilt when we are feeling sadness or deep grief, and oddly enough we can similarly feel guilty for being extremely happy or content. Guilt has the uncanny ability to make us question our right to even feel joy, if we know someone else may not be experiencing similar exuberance at the same time. Here, if you allow yourself the permission to delve deeper, you'll have your first dawning, your first awakening from the lie we have all been living and from that which has been causing such confusion and suffering ...

No matter how hard your attempts are made to eradicate guilt, they will always be in vain.

Attempting to eradicate that which feels very real, very 'at home' within us, but which is actually not real at all, will always be attempts made in vain. Guilt is only real to the extent that we make it so. Guilt is real, only because we have made a home for it within our consciousness. Guilt is real, only because we were shown *how* to accommodate it. Guilt is real, only because we were conditioned and programmed to be so accepting of it.

If you are to experience a guilt-free existence and relieve yourself of its stranglehold, then the unnatural and weirdly concocted phenomenon you have unconsciously made of it, is to be dropped from your consciousness altogether. That's quite different from trying to eradicate it or making yourself feel better about it.

Instead, you must see it for the lie about your Life that it is. See where it comes from, how much it controls and how much it is used to manipulate and diminish your character. As you do so, you will begin to realise the extent to which you have been living in servitude to ignorance. Guilt is purely an illusion brought on by our misunderstanding of Who We Truly Are. This will become more clear to you as you read on and as you re-member and re-claim truths once kept hidden about your very Self. For now, simply breathe and become aware that guilt does not have to continue imprisoning you for the rest of your days.

REVELATION. *Guilt was not a thought or feeling you possessed when you came into the world. The experience of guilt had to be described and demonstrated to you, taught and expected of you, before it could take root in your own experience. Guilt serves no benefit, other than to keep you feeling inferior and apologetic. We can even feel guilt activated within us about something that has had nothing directly to do with us at all. Guilt is always destructive.*

REALISATION. *You have reached a point in your Life, when many of the beliefs and acceptances you have been living no longer feel true for you or possible to continue holding. Perhaps they never did but until* NOW *you may have felt even more guilty for daring to no longer feel guilty! This book is not deciding anything new for you. It has come into your Life when you needed to be re-affirmed that the guilt you have been carrying, cannot possibly serve any Life-giving purpose. Guilt will always make you feel less than whole, less than worthy, less than fully alive. The great realisation here then is ... there can be Life without guilt. Ponder that truth* NOW *and ask yourself; Would I feel more or less complete, if I were to be without guilt? Remember, no one else is living* YOUR *Life, only you can decide for you.*

METANOIA. *Take a generous breath in now and as you exhale, know that already and in this moment, you are releasing the illusionary construct the burden of guilt is. Take a second deep breath and, as you exhale, feel the permission you've not been given before and the authority you have at last granted to yourself, to let guilt leave your consciousness, forever. Take a third refreshing intake of breath and, as you exhale, know that it is perfectly* OK *to grant yourself your new-found freedom. No one else has the authority to do that for you. So call off the need to remain in waiting for anyone else to grant you their approval and read on ...*

CHAPTER TWO

Questioning your purpose

Until you make the unconscious conscious, it will direct your Life and you will call it fate.

–Carl G. Jung

Why do you believe what you believe? This is a question that many people are ill-equipped to answer, because they have been taught it should never be asked. For many, faith is sufficient, even the faith to have 'blind faith'. Experience is the authority to which many appeal, putting complete trust in the long existing authorities that have always been operating; religions, law enforcers, judiciaries, governing bodies, education systems, health advisors, financial institutions, and every other authoritative system you can name. The biggest authoritative imprint of all, being made on us by our parents—for better or for worse. You might say, we have all learned to blindly accept the 'traditions' that have regulated our ways of collectively conforming; socially, orderly, morally, obediently, lawfully. Tradition makes sure that we don't stray far from the thoughts, customs and ways of the past. Often our most cherished beliefs are grounded in little more than fear of what the consequences would otherwise be, if we were to abandon them.

Into such a mix of certainty and uncertainty, conviction and confusion has ventured the book you are now reading. Why are you reading it? Same reason it was written. Because for most of your Life, if not all of it, you may never have felt you were fully living your own truth. That is, living your Life in complete alignment with Life itself, and living it with great freedom, without having to make sure that any choices, decisions and actions of your own had first received approval from some other channel of authority.

Could your experience have been any different for you? Could you have been living without the need to feel so monitored by that which is sometimes called your conscience? It is unlikely. Guilt and your psyche have become so interwoven and inextricably linked with shame, depression, suppression, remorse, regret, blame, sin, punishment, contrition, along with depictions of Heaven and Hell, that you must be absolutely determined to escape its debilitating grasp, if you are to reclaim complete freedom of heart, spirit, mind and will.

Until you drop guilt from your consciousness, it can only continue to cause prolonged suffering, sometimes spilling over into self-loathing, self-harm, addictive behaviours and unworthiness. Accommodating guilt will ensure your Life is kept at a very low frequency vibration. At such a low vibration, you can only wallow in fear. When you are in fear you become dependent, hopeful, wishful, perhaps at best prayerful or at worst even pleading, but all the time in servitude. Most human beings view Life from a 'victim mentality' and guilt is always at the core of such mentality. The leap of consciousness required to 'slip out' from victim mentality is sometimes referred to as the act of re-claiming your own personal sovereignty. Psychiatrist, Carl Gustav Jung described that leap as making "the unconscious conscious" and you are now at the doorstep, ready to make that shift in your own consciousness. The desire of your Soul no longer feels it possible to needlessly be peering out at Life, as if from behind iron bars.

Know this and become aware ...

As you give yourself permission to question the absurdity of guilt, which has kept you in such a diminished existence, awareness of your own personal sovereignty gradually starts to emerge.

All the time, just keep asking yourself;

What has been keeping me from living my own truth,
and why have I been trying to live somebody else's version of it?
And, by making the responsible decision to live my own truth,
how differently can I now enjoy Life with a free
heart, a free spirit, a free mind and a free will?

Perhaps a helpful way to demonstrate just how ridiculous the lie of guilt can be, is to take a sample snap shot of the multiplicity of ways it adversely affects us. We can frequently experience waves of guilt arising in us, even though they are most often entirely mis-placed. They arise, simply because of the programming of our human condition. Your struggles with guilt were not present when you came into this world, that's for sure, and now you are more consciously aware of that. Guilt was systematically implanted and its disturbing affect can even arise within you for things you've never done! You may be surprised to find that some of your own experiences of guilt are, oddly enough, very common. Once you become aware of this, it should at very least make you raise an eyebrow, or even bring about a burst of laughter from within when you recognise how much so many of us are affected by the same things. Why on earth would you continue to give space to that which we call guilt and to the needless turbulence it brings about?

For example ...
Have you ever immediately put both hands back on the steering wheel of your car, when only one hand had been there before, just because a police car pulled up alongside you at the traffic lights? Or taken an immediate glance at your phone on the seat next to you, feeling a wave of guilt passing through you just for it being there? Or, maybe started to worry about failing a breathalyser when you haven't even been drinking?

Have you ever felt the uneasy sense of guilt as you approach a customs barrier at the airport, even though you have never smuggled anything in your Life before and had no intention of doing it this time?

What about times when a family member or a friend has held a different point of view or has a different perspective from you. How often can guilt be stirred in you for not sharing their more dominant perspective?

Then, there's guilt which can arise in you by association. Perhaps you've experienced that discomfort if you found yourself sitting in a public place, a coffee shop, bar, or restaurant and when someone in your company is speaking out loud and inappropriately about someone else? Have you ever had the feeling of guilt being stirred within you, in case someone else in that place thought you were also being bigoted or disingenuous? Perhaps your discomfort was so great that you felt like apologising to the waitress for putting up with the disturbance, even though it was not you at the cause of it!

What about the classic example of having a baby or toddler crying or having a tantrum and all eyes are only on YOU? Or at least that's how you may have felt!

Someone has misplaced something and you join in the search, looking for it everywhere, but still can't help them find it. What happens then, when guilt surfaces and your mind tells you they may not have believed you? Or worse, that they may have thought YOU had taken it! This same scenario goes in reverse too. When you have lost something and just *know* someone has stolen it, only to find it afterwards, and then feeling guilty for having had that thought!

Perhaps you selected a movie to watch with your family and, unexpectedly, a sex scene appears on the screen, you feel uncomfortable about the choice you'd made, even though you'd not ever seen the movie before!

Have you ever had the unpleasant experience of being in an elevator or on a plane where someone has passed wind, making a sound or leaving an unwanted smell? A bad odour left behind is never a nice experience, but nothing like as bad as feeling guilt that others may have thought it was you!

Every one of us can relate to these experiences and you will be able to think of so many more, similar in kind. Innocuous as they are, they still bring about a feeling of unease. They still make us feel small, apologetic, disconnected, and very much *in the wrong*. These are the instances guilt makes as its most regular habitat. In more extreme experiences, the intensity of guilt we feel can skyrocket.

The more devastating examples of guilt of course, are those that literally have you feeling 'racked'. They are those which have plunged you into deep pain and daily suffering for things of the past. They are the experiences of guilt which most likely attracted you to read this book.

Violations committed against another, which may already have been punished by the law courts but still haunt you long after you've served your sentence, are often at the root of the more insidious aspects of guilt. This is when no severity of sentence pronounced or penalty paid, no amount of purging undergone or forgiveness sought, no amount of repentance or contrition made, can feel sufficient enough to release you from guilt's dominion. And so the daily mental onslaught you inflict on yourself keeps you as victim and prisoner to guilt.

Again, such examples of guilt's vast trawl of possible scenarios and instances could not all be counted or specifically identified in these pages - nor is it necessary to do so - because every person reading this book will now be thinking primarily of their own experiences of it. Most often of course, you're the only one who can be truly aware just how much you've been affected by your own experiences, because guilt is a highly personalised phenomenon. When you hold guilt in your mind and in your heart, it is an assault made by yourself on yourself. It is to literally be at war with your very Being.

As you read further on into this book, all of the time becoming more consciously aware, many more revelations and realisations about guilt - once hidden from you - will become more obvious to you. Then it will be up to you to decide, if you want to live a Life of freedom, or one that continues to be guilt ridden.

Know this and become aware ...

You cannot have both.
You will not experience the freedom you desire
in this Life-time while carrying guilt.
For one is mutually exclusive of the other.

Guilt can stem from a multiplicity of things. It can range from crimes of murder and fatalities, caused deliberately or by negligence, to relatively innocuous experiences. It can even be the aftermath of sheer accidents which you have continued to relentlessly blame yourself for. It can be felt where there has been infidelity in marriage or unfaithfulness between partners, often described as "cheating" or "being cheated". Parents will regularly experience the pain of guilt for times when their off-spring went on to make choices or decisions that were in conflict with those of their own. They will feel they should have guided them differently. And, parents will hold onto guilt for things they said or didn't say to their children, ruing the various ways they may have neglected or mistreated them. At the birth of twins, when only one child survives and its twin does not, guilt can lie heavily on the child who lives on, knowing their twin did not.

Guilt, however, is at its most intense when the 'God' relationship we may have formed feels like it is in jeopardy. Those with religious convictions, will be the more likely to feel the anguish and torment of that, and we will explore the anguish presented by this dilemma in later chapters.

Everyone reading this book will have their own personal experiences of guilt. There will be those experiences which are so personalised to you that you may feel no one else could possibly understand them. You may also feel that no words could adequately explain them, and you may simply feel too fearful, ashamed or embarrassed to share with others, that which is causing you such deep pangs of guilt.

All the while, in whichever form your pain or shame arises, it is vital to keep in your awareness that guilt is not a natural aspect of our humanity. Guilt is a man-made, mind-made lie about Life. Humanity has adopted guilt and consented to it, and we have all forgotten that. Guilt is borrowed and it is borrowed from those who have not questioned, released or transcended it. It is also used by some to manipulate and control, knowing how vulnerable guilt makes us feel. In turn, we have all learned to use guilt destructively to feed the ego. It will often have been achieved by personifying a false sense of dominion over others and, by doing so, alerting guilt in another when they don't feel they can be just as forceful. Conversely, it can also be by keeping ourselves in a 'locked down' reality about our own right to feel worthy, or as the equal to anyone else. However, no matter how dominant the ego, the presence of guilt will always keep you so much smaller than if you were to be without it. Guilt has no empowering qualities and no Life-giving purpose to offer, and it will never allow you the ease to feel that you rightfully belong in your own body. Guilt will obscure the unique presence you are here to be, because guilt does not naturally belong within us.

Know this and become aware ...

For as long as past hurts are not healed, brought closure to and resolved, they remain as present and then future sufferings.

Guilt which most often underlies and accompanies your pain, and which usually is supported like two book-ends by shame and blame, can be so deeply ingrained that it feels hard to ever be fully accepting of yourself. It can also erase from your mind the possibility that you could ever again be acceptable to others. Once you begin to doubt your self-worth to this degree, never feeling that you truly 'belong', a whole torrent of claustrophobic experiences line up to re-enforce and convince your mind that you must have been RIGHT in your self-condemnation!

Suppression, repression, depression and addiction are all symptomatic of the sense of disconnection you can experience when guilt is in the driving seat. Life can seem little more than a constant series of challenges and pit-falls, where you are forever trying to prove yourself, in order to be deserving of it! As a result, you remain caught up in a web of confusion and unrest; feeling powerless to find the peace of heart and mind you so much crave.

Whatever has kept you so loyal to the destructive 'idea' about yourself, which guilt is, must now be abandoned. No-thing from your past can continue to negatively dominate your present, unless it is attached to the notion of guilt. Awareness of this is your key to freedom. Each page you read of this book will feel good, because its message is to remind you of your true essence. Every sentence will resonate with your Soul, because the truth your mind had temporarily forgotten, your heart and will are now excited to re-instate.

REVELATION. *Because we are each energised by the same Source which energises everything else, you will always find your joy in those you share this Life with. This is why the relationships we forge in Life are so important. We look to find in others that which we know already resides in each of us; love and acceptance. As we find it, we again feel that we belong and no longer seem disconnected. Guilt falsely creates a sense of separation between yourself and others and between your heart and the rest of your physiology. When you feel disconnected from your heart, you feel you are not truly living and, indeed you are not. At best, you are merely dying to live!*

REALISATION. *We all have a yearning to feel constantly connected to Source. We know we 'belong' and, at a cellular level, we know that something larger forms ultimate reality. We do not always have the vocabulary to explain or adequately express it, but we feel certain that there is so much more going on than our own individual experience would tell us. You know, at a deeper level, that you are part of all this, that you are an Individuation of the Divine. Until now, you may not have chosen to describe yourself as that, but you still know it to be so!*

METANOIA. *Follow your aliveness! This is the most profound expression of metanoia. Life is beckoning you to be the unique presence in the world you were born to be. It will not matter how you may have erred or what mistakes you have made. To be restored to whole-heartedness is what is on offer here, regardless of the depth of pain guilt has had your mind internally re-playing. Apology to another for pain caused to them may not always be possible. It may not even be accepted by them. That does not mean, however, that you remain imprisoned by guilt. Another person's forgiveness is not what is ultimately needed for you to be free. Forgiveness of yourself is all that's necessary. Then you can move on in peace.*

CHAPTER THREE

Awakening from the wound of duality

There is no polite way to tell people they've dedicated their lives to an illusion.

–Daniel Dennett

Thanks to the world we live in, we've developed many habits that are the direct result of living almost exclusively 'in-ego', rather than from the radiance of our true essence. When we are living exclusively in ego, we are living in ignorance; being kept 'in the dark' so to speak. Remember ... you are so much more than the mind structured egoic identity formed about you.

The ego only comes out for you to see, in the same way ignorance of your true Self only becomes clear to you, once it is exposed to the glaring headlights of awareness. You are now shedding light on the nonsense which guilt is, so that you may become more consciously aware of the ignorance you've been unconsciously locked into. Ego and guilt make a close-knit partnership and they keep us very much 'in the dark'. The more aware you become, the more you begin to realise that the ego is part of you, but it is not who you are. As soon as you make space for that revelation to become your new realisation, you are becoming more consciously aware. By taking responsibility for your state of consciousness in the moment, you interrupt ignorance and *metanoia* is at once made possible.

Awareness enables you to see that the ego is just a series of concepts and judgments to start with—descriptions or stories strung together to formulate your false sense of self. The thinking mind, with its sole ability to process data through the concept of the ego, can only perceive things in relation to this ego. Ego and the thinking mind, therefore, become indistinguishable. This is why there is no language you can use to describe an event you have encountered without in some way, explicitly or implicitly, referencing it to yourself.

So, for example, a common attribute many of our egos possess is the idea that we are 'stressed' or, in some way 'unhappy'. Ego then goes about reinforcing this inner sense of unease paradoxically by trying to avoid feeling 'stressed' or 'unhappy'. It does this by going out of its way to deny many of the feelings that are generated inside when we encounter difficult situations. We all do it. Rather than simply sitting with the pain we are feeling when something doesn't go our way (as is often the case), we immediately go into avoidance mode; almost as if we are initiating a form of anaesthesia! We start keeping ourselves busy, we think, we act, we talk, we do whatever we can to zone out. However, the more we indulge these actions, the more inflamed our ego becomes, and the vicious cycle goes on, generating more stress and more unhappiness. Instead, all that is necessary in those situations is to remain very still.

When you are still, the presence of your true Self replaces the ego's reactionary mayhem. All it takes to make this transition is the time to stop, consciously breathe, and bring awareness to the experience in your body which has mentally undergone such an onslaught. Then, simply by giving your mind and body some space and time to recover from the ego's reactionary impulse, awareness begins to naturally arise within you. Panic subsides and any pain can begin to diminish or be completely dissolved.

Guilt is so interwoven with the ego, we mistakenly believe it to be the sum total of who we are. As you become more aware, you will observe that one of the jobs of the ego's reactionary impulses is to make yourself, or someone else, feel guilty. Another of its jobs is to blame others. You may often have found yourself or will hear other people exclaiming things like; "Look what you made me do!", or, "How can you still be mad at me after I bought you that lovely gift?", or, "I should have done something and I didn't", or, "I wish I'd never been born", or, "You're upsetting my mother", or, "You always make me feel so guilty", or, "Stop loading the guilt on me".

All of these expressions, and many others like it, strengthen your sense of ego-identification and there is no stronger ego than the negative one. This is where you repeatedly condemn or diminish yourself, or another, for something from the past. Guilt will often support the ego's negative condemnation of a past hurt, or a difference there was between two people, by infusing a situation arising in the present with the same negativity. This egoic drive creates immense confusion, duality, and it has us all constantly making divisions in our mind, illusionary as they are. For example, the ego distinguishes between its perceived idea of 'self' as if separate from 'another'. It also makes up the idea of 'self', as if it were possible to even exist in total separation from the Source of Life that sources everything.

This book is more interested in the *truth* of non-duality or 'Advaita', which simply means 'not two'. Advaita is the Sanskrit word meaning wholeness, completeness, unity. It points to an intimacy right at the heart of present moment experience, a love beyond words which exists right now, prior to any apparent separation. Advaita, non-duality, points us back Home. Of course, we all *know* Advaita, we have just forgotten to remember it!

Advaita was our experience as we were birthed into this world. As you emerged from your mother's birth canal, you instinctively knew how to move through it, how to swim. Your connectivity with the Source of Life ensured your safety. Long before you were taught *how to* swim you were already doing it! Long before you were taught *how to* 'do' Life, you were already living it ... breathing, communicating, feeding, interacting. You are Life and Life is You!

Know this and become aware ...

Never have you been disconnected from the Source of Life and never will you experience separation from it.

The ways you have been conditioned to think and act and behave have formed the ego. How you have become programmed and the ways you've been shown to 'do' Life have combined to create the illusion of separateness from it, duality. Now, in truth, it is not possible for any human being to be content and experience wholeness, completeness and unity, until we free ourselves from much of that which has been led within us. Misinformation, indoctrination, confusion - along with our own illusions - have all contributed to fashion the ego-identification formed within each of us. They combine to create a sense of incompleteness and disunity. At the same time, the potency of our true essence, Advaita, has systematically been erased from our memory bank. Ignorance of your true Self has had you imprisoned in a *locked down* reality. You've very much been kept in the dark, and this is where guilt thrives most strongly.

Now, suppressed as your mind has become by the programmed ways you've been exposed to, you *know* deep down inside that there is so much more to your Self than how you've been instructed and influenced. The fact you have purposely sought out this book and are reading it now, is indication of that.

You *know* that guilt is getting in the way of what otherwise would be your natural connection with Life itself; your sense of wholeness, completeness, unity.

You *know* that there was a time when you were without guilt And, despite the compelling appearance of separation and diversity which guilt stirs within you, you know that oneness is all there is—and you are included.

You *know* duality - that odd notion of separateness you've been trying to live out - has always left you feeling 'incomplete'.

You *know* that guilt has never made any sense.

You *know* it does not naturally belong within you.

You also *know* that no amount of guilt can make any positive difference whatsoever, to that which you *believed* you should be feeling guilty about!

Yet, the ego has made a home for guilt and the mind will use it to convince you that you are always living in separation. It will have you splitting everything into opposites, convincing you that 'good' and 'bad', 'right' and 'wrong' are absolutes, and that there is a gap between you and the Source of Life that sources everything. The ego has created the idea of 'Redeemer' and those yet to be 'Redeemed'.

In the next chapters, we will trace some of the most significant impacts and influences to have kept humanity as conditioned and programmed as it is. In particular, we need to examine the enormous influence of religion, its projection of morality, its fear mongering dogmas and excessive demands for conformity. We also need to see where else in our societies and cultures similar kinds of constraint have been imposed by other coercive institutions. Authoritative organisations and establishments which determine for us what is acceptable, or even permissible, and what is not, are rarely questioned enough by us.

Even the education systems, which we are duty bound to send our children to and which are principally established to teach right from wrong and good from bad, are also capable of diminishing self-confidence and self-worth, while instilling guilt, shame or a sense of failure. So many of our authoritative bodies are rooted in the illusion of duality and, albeit often unconsciously, they contribute to a systematic dismantling of our personal sovereignty and minimise the purpose and potency of our existence. As you are reading this right now, you will know exactly which destructive influences and impacts negatively affected you when you made your own transition through childhood and then into adulthood. Guilt and shame had to be imposed from some external force, and Life is inviting you to put the spotlight on where those irrational and excessive demands for conformity came from. Now that you are an adult, and becoming more consciously aware, the time has come to interrupt your programming and to reconsider the value those influences were to you. They will have had a considerable affect on your development and still influence your decisions today.

For some people, the decision to leave a religious practice behind after many years, or to make some other big turn around from that which once brought comfort, uplift, or fulfilment, may seem too daunting to even contemplate. It may also never be necessary. However, if you have a commitment, obligation or allegiance to anyone or to anything which no longer feels congruent, whether it be to a religion, or adherence to a system, or to a person you have a relationship with, then think again. You must always be prepared to go beyond your ordinary way of thinking and seeing, if you are to accept that there may be relationships you were once dedicated to, that were actually founded on control and ownership, not equality and mutual respect.

With any allegiance or relationship, the power to control and the ego's drive to possess will always thrive most strongly and dominate if you present as dependent or needy. Your guilt will ensure that. This is evident when a couple feel bound by wedding vows ... "for better or worse, for richer for poorer, in sickness and in health, till death do us part", but then find they can no longer sustain that Life-long commitment with joy and freedom. In that scenario, it is imperative not to allow obligation, and the feeling of guilt which sits behind it, to crush heart, spirit, mind and will. Though guilt most usually wins out, misery will be the inevitable outcome.

Guilt is the means by which humanity has been kept blinkered to our magnitude. As the philosopher, writer, and cognitive scientist Daniel Dennett neatly puts it ... we have all been "dedicated to an illusion". Desperate as you may be to release whatever guilt you are holding, and though your desire to be free of it may at times be overwhelming, you may well feel more afraid, more guilty, if you were to simply dump guilt from your consciousness than if you continued to just hang onto it. We have indeed become hypnotised by and dedicated to an illusion!

Now, you've got to admit, it must have taken some brainwashing to reach that state of confusion and to be stuck in that kind of dilemma! However, in all likelihood, that's exactly the confused state the notion of guilt and your accommodation of it has brought you to. To make you feel a little better about your reluctance to shed that which has been so destructive, you might be relieved to hear that you're certainly not alone in having reached this state of confusion. It is so common in fact, that there is even a recognised terminology for what you are experiencing. It is known as cognitive dissonance. Be alert to the fact that cognitive dissonance is likely going on within you in this very moment. This is how psychiatrist, philosopher, and revolutionary Frantz Fanon describes the in-built protectiveness and resistance to change which cognitive dissonance, psychologically, brings up inside of us. It keeps us loyal to the deceptiveness of the ego, causing us to mentally and emotionally shut down and disregard any rational evidence that contradicts what we previously regarded as absolute 'truth' ...

"Sometimes people hold a core belief that is very strong. When they are presented with evidence that works against that belief, the new evidence cannot be accepted. It would create a feeling that is extremely uncomfortable, called cognitive dissonance. And because it is so important to protect the core belief, they will rationalise, ignore and even deny anything that doesn't fit in with the core belief."

Know this and become aware ...

**... Your heart and Soul may feel more than ready
to free yourself from guilt's stranglehold**

**... The words of this book will be resonating
excitedly with your inner-knowing at the
prospect of experiencing instant freedom**

**... But, your learned and well-practised illusion of
imprisonment - courtesy of the ego - will do all in its
power to stall and thwart the process of your liberation.**

Naturally, your mind works according to its old conditioning and humanity has well and truly been conditioned by the repeatedly programmed core beliefs instilled within us. The majority of those beliefs being formed before the age of 7-8 years old. Not surprisingly, those early formative years of our childhood are known as the 'imprint' years; for that is precisely when and how those who most strongly and consistently influence us, imprint their own long held core beliefs. Our learned beliefs soon become our repetitive programmed behaviours. They largely remain unquestioned and soon become cemented, fixed. We continue living our lives in accordance with them, as if they were absolute truths. It is how we learn to interpret and perceive reality. It is how we believe Life to be. It is how we form the egoic identification of who we *think* we are.

To be freed from your conditioned thinking and to wake up to the realisation that you are so much more than the ego-self formed *about* you, you have to recognise when the thoughts you have 'borrowed' from others are driving you. Importantly, you must also be aware that they stem from the core beliefs that were imprinted on you. If they are liberating, they will serve you well and you will always feel in alignment with Life. If they are limiting, they will always have you feeling disconnected from Life, perhaps even undeserving of it. This is when guilt becomes more deeply seated.

In order to experience your inner desire for freedom, you need to cultivate the necessary proficiency to be the 'watcher' of all that is going on inside of you. Once you become proficient at 'watching' your conditioned programming, you will be able to observe and monitor the accumulated thoughts and the imprinted core beliefs which are always running on auto-pilot mode. You will see that they are governing every one of your choices and decisions. Your programming will have been doing this for you, for better or for worse, whether you were conscious of it or not. Now, with greater awareness, you will be able to *watch* and then be more selective of the thoughts and beliefs you choose to keep and those you let go of. As the observer, you will be empowered to steer your programmed ego beyond the gravitational pull of guilt - which is totally dependent on egoic identification - and which has been keeping you rooted in ignorance of your true Self.

In the moment of realisation that your thoughts, generated by the ego, are structural and not content based, they begin to lose their power over you. They will try to return, because the ego never settles easily if it has been thwarted, but you will now be so much better equipped to deal with those same thoughts when they do unsettle you again. Now your awareness will be more alert, more watchful, more observant. And, once you have understood the deceptiveness of the ego, once you have become more consciously aware of the imprisonment it has had you locked into, you will be more present as the 'watcher' of your thoughts and as the selector and decision-maker of your imprinted core beliefs. You will instantly realise that a thought is only a thought, you don't have to continue thinking it! You will realise that a belief is only a belief, here today gone tomorrow, you don't have to continue believing it! With that awareness, you have at your disposal the most potent transformational tool; potent enough to override the ego and dissolve programmed thoughts and conditioned core beliefs that have not been serving you well. You will now have the consciousness powerful enough to diffuse cognitive dissonance, and bring you back into alignment with your true, Advaita, Self.

Life is inviting you to see everything through a new lens and with a free heart, without the burden of guilt. By accepting Life's invitation, you will inevitably experience a paradigm shift where old assumptions and beliefs are seen to be false and no longer applicable. You will enter a completely new and fresh way of living; alert and aware rather than worried or fearful; responsive rather than reactive; empowered rather than disempowered; in the flow of Life rather than up against it; charged with the wisdom to make more enlightened choices and decisions; no longer buried in guilt, filled with shame, or stunted by remorse.

Your natural desire for freedom is now being re-ignited. Life often intervenes if we are not getting a realisation quickly enough, and you have had to be interrupted, awakened, in order to evolve.

REVELATION. *Life is always changing and so are you! You have now reached a point when it feels time to experience an inner revolution; a radical change in how you view reality. That change is being stirred not so much by you, but from within you. Had things been left to the ego, very little would change. However, you are an Individuation of the Divine. You have an ego, but it is not the sum total of who you are. Your spirit is literally moving you on.*

REALISATION. *It is time to stop believing what your mind tells you. Nothing your mind tells you is true, nothing your mind tells you is real. Nothing. Observe your mind in the same way you might read a storybook. Laugh, enjoy but do not believe it. The only difference between your readiness to release guilt and the person still buried in it, is that you now know where your doubts come from. You know they are the result of conditioning.*

METANOIA. *Say to yourself this wonderful mantra to accelerate the freedom you desire— "I have arrived. I am home, in the here and now." This mantra begins the process of looking inward rather than outward. It is a move from insanity to sanity, from relying on the external world for the permission to experience freedom, to recognising your own inner personal sovereignty. This applies whatever your external circumstances may be; whether you are reading this book from a prison cell and serving a sentence for past crimes, or whether you are in a monastic cell pleading for God's forgiveness for past sins. Guilt forms its stranglehold differently for every individual, but always has the same destructive outcome —it keeps us fastened in victim mentality. Metanoia is the experience of being present, allowing a deep, pervasive sense of peace to become apparent. It is a sense of coming home to a place you never actually left. It's becoming aware that only guilt was keeping this inner revolution out of your reach and only guilt that was keeping your never-ending struggle intact.*

CHAPTER FOUR

Victim mentality: Blame and shame

We're here to awaken from the illusion of separateness.

—Ram Dass

Everyone is afraid of change and everyone has a natural ability to adapt but why, then, is it so hard for us to adapt to feelings of happiness, satisfaction and completeness? We resist these beautiful emotions because guilt tells us that we are unworthy of them, that they cannot possibly last. In truth, it is guilt that stops the natural healthy flow of e-motion, (energy in motion).

The nature of emotion is that we always experience it as spontaneous. Emotions are temporary, yet ever flowing through us and out of us, in response to how each situation makes us feel. Our interpretation of how we *should* feel and how we *should* react to situations as they arise has, of course, also been conditioned and programmed.

Know this and become aware ...

As a child, you will never intentionally have done anything *wrong* but you will often have discovered from the reaction of others that you must have!

Tragically, that false idea about yourself, imprinted by others, has become the 'idea' you've continued to live out ever since. Not surprisingly, the confusion you have experienced, while trying to make sense of that mixed-bag of imprinted philosophies, ideologies, beliefs, thoughts and opinions has created much uncertainty, doubt and insecurity within you.

Insecurity is inbred in each of us. Guilt sees to it that we live our lives in the 'hope' we'll get through it, in the 'possibility' we'll survive it, and in the 'wish' that the choices and decisions we make, *might* receive approval from others. And, whether you consider yourself to have a belief in a 'God' or not, guilt also sees to it that the ultimate authority you have sought the approval of and permission from, has only felt sufficient when granted by an external source. We either look to a 'Higher Power', a deity we've fashioned, that not one of us can see but have still learned to fear, or we remain in deference to some other person or authority to the same degree. It's a 'victim mentality'. We can do this with certain key figures in our lives, often it is our parents. We can become victims to a relationship we feel bound by, or to money, property, land, material possessions, a job, a position or to a role we play out. We can also revere and rarely think to question the decisions made for us by banks, governments, health authorities, medical practitioners, education systems and the like. Our total reliance on 'blind faith' alone to *get us through Life,* is precisely the cause of our every confusion and our enormous insecurity. At best, a victim mentality will have you tiptoeing through Life in a state of wishful thinking. At worst, it will have you living Life in abject fear and neediness, frightened that your prayers and wishes may go forever unheard.

Guilt has created an illusionary gap between creator and all that is created; a divide between ourselves and the Source of Life that sources everything. In turn, duality has formed a depiction of Life which leaves us feeling vulnerable, fragile and disconnected. It has prompted you to become uncertain of your essence, doubtful of your purpose, unworthy and fear-filled.

Guilt has instilled an *idea* of the Divine, more akin to a court of law, and religious depictions have consistently presented the 'God' figure as the supreme authority presiding over 'His' court. Religions, almost always, present their 'God' as a masculine persona. They have taken the exact same image and terminology we use to describe our judicial systems to then create and impose a fictitious image of a deity, separate from humanity in 'His' interaction with us, and as one who stands as judge over us. Consequently, we live our lives in a perpetual state of anxiety; frightened by the thought we might get Life 'wrong', and fearful of being judged and sentenced for it.

The deep pain you suffer, the insecurity you feel, the anxiety and uncertainties you fear are all, of course, the result of being sucked into the illusion of duality. The shame felt, in the belief it could even be possible for you to be alienated from your Source, has you blaming and judging yourself. Self recrimination keeps a victim mentality fuelled and further feeds the illusion that it is possible for you to lose connection with your Source.

Know this and become aware ...

> **The imprisonment of guilt you endure creates a 'victim mentality'. In the mistaken belief that you are automatically severed from your Source for a 'wrong doing' committed, shame becomes deeply embedded in your unconscious mind.**

The *real* lie that you have been living is your submission to a distorted notion about your very Being: inferior, helpless and powerless, totally dependent on the mercy and leniency of an external authority. Such indoctrination has systematically eroded all sense of your personal sovereignty. Instead, you shallow breath your way through Life, always suspecting you are culpable of doing something deemed to be so unforgivable, that the hammer may unexpectedly be slammed down in judgment at the end of your trial, pronouncing you: "GUILTY" as charged.

Our psyche has become branded with the impression of an authority outside of ourselves - often invisible to us - but always watching our every move and ready to judge. So powerful is that branded impression, that even when we choose not to use the term 'God', the same overriding thinking permeates the whole fabric of our existence and dominates our heart, spirit, mind and will.

Human beings have come to perceive everything and everyone in our environment as a possible threat. It is almost impossible to cultivate positive attitudes and beliefs when we are always stuck in survival mode. The fear that we could possibly get Life 'wrong' means we become overwhelmed with excessive stress, and that our every experience becomes a series of short-term emergencies. We lose the ability to relax and enjoy the moment. We live from crisis to crisis, with little or no relief in sight. For some people, burnout or physical, mental, emotional and spiritual breakdown is inevitable. This may well have been your own experience. It may also have been the overwhelming sense of disconnection, alienation or aloneness felt by you, that has propelled you to read this book.

Now, Life is inviting you to return to your more natural state of alignment and, through the 3-fold process of REVELATION - REALISATION - METANOIA, you can begin to re-instate your own personal sovereignty and begin to live your Life as the Individuation of the Divine you truly are. The process is an unfolding of consciousness. It is a process of *remembering* the truth of who you really are. From your new realisations, emerges the freedom to take full responsibility for your existence as well as the awareness, emotional intelligence, self-forgiveness and empathy necessary, to make choices and decisions from an unburdened heart, an unburdened spirit, an unburdened mind and an unburdened will.

As you begin again to experience Advaita - non-duality - many new discoveries will fall into place and you will immediately feel the difference of no longer being up against Life. Your Life will be so much more complete, when you no longer feel compelled to prove yourself to be worthy of it. In guilt, it never seems that you feel 'good' enough, or can be 'forgiven' enough, 'deserving' enough, 'acceptable' enough. The victim mentality required to keep guilt firmly in place and the effort of living from day to day in the 'hope' of being accepted, is a miserable experience of Life. It is the polar opposite to Life lived in Advaita.

Because guilt creates the illusion of duality, blame becomes the ego's most automatic reaction to the intolerable threat you fear of being separated from your Source. It is also the panic of possible non-acceptance by others. Whenever you feel you are in separation from Life itself or potentially alienated from others and alone, your body is triggered into the stress response mode, most often called 'fight or flight'. As you feel yourself being sucked into that state of panic, you immediately resort to blaming someone or something else for your discomfort. Instantly, your unconscious mind has you scanning and searching your environment, looking for the 'enemy' to point the finger at and to blame. Blame is the body's spontaneously activated response to the discomfort you feel and to the possible threat of feeling ashamed. In a split second, the area of your brain called the hypothalamus initiates a sequence of nerve cell firing, and chemicals like adrenaline, noradrenaline and cortisol are released into your bloodstream to physically and psychologically make ready for defence.

Your in-built reaction to blame, when those situations arise, is to preserve your self-esteem. Blame, however, is a fearful kick-back response of the ego, which completely prevents you from taking personal responsibility for the decisions you make, or the situations and circumstances you encounter. Your heart is not open. Your rational mind is disengaged. Your consciousness is focused on fear, not love, and your personal sovereignty is all but extinguished as you rapidly lose sight of your connectivity to Source.

Sometimes, this feeling of disconnection can actually serve you well in the long term. Many people literally experience that the magnitude of their discomfort usually provides motivation enough to re-examine their beliefs, values and goals. However, unless you uproot guilt from your psyche altogether and truly see it as the unnecessary imprisonment you have got so much used to, then much of your existence will continue to be lived in the stress response mode. You will continue to go day after day in this alert state, bypassing your rational mind—where your more well thought out beliefs exist—and move into 'attack' mode, blaming others or blaming yourself and then feeling ashamed about your impulsive reactions. As a result, guilt becomes even more deeply embedded. The automatic 'fight or flight' stress response exaggerates your fears and distorts your thinking, always taking you back into your programming and to your conditioned ways. You see everything through the filter of possible danger and narrow your focus down to everything you believed could harm you. Inevitably fear continues to be the lens through which you see the world.

Blame is the desperate attempt to relieve ourselves from the discomfort of guilt. It is also the panic reaction to hide our feelings of helplessness which, even if only momentary and passing, are totally uncomfortable for us to bear. Blame is the tool we instinctively use to fend off shame or, more specifically, to prevent the feeling of being 'ashamed'. At very least, blame is an attempt to feel less on our own. And yet, the irony of the reaction to blame depends totally on maintaining the erroneous belief that it could ever be possible for you to be 'cut off' from the Source of Life. Only if you are to keep that erroneous belief and keep with the depiction of a 'God' - an external authority - who is out to get you for things done 'wrong', will you continue to be dogged by the experience of guilt.

Know this and become aware ...

Your experience of guilt is the result of the beliefs you've held. Guilt is dependent on duality and guilt breeds a victim mentality. Guilt is required to keep shame and the feeling of being ashamed firmly in place.

If you were to remain in a situation, whether in a relationship, a place of work, part of an organisation or in a religion or Church where you have to watch every word you say, or follow irrelevant rules and demands, then you can never be happy. Guilt may be keeping you feeling duty bound to an unfulfilling relationship or to some other commitment or allegiance and, whenever that is the case, you will resort to blaming others or yourself for your perceived helplessness.

As you become more consciously aware that the play of guilt, blame and shame are at work in all of these scenarios, and many more, you awaken to a new truth. You realise that the path you may have felt obligated to, rather than satisfyingly connected to, is a path made of eggshells. It may also be the dawning that it is not the path for you any more.

REVELATION. *The most important wisdom of all, is the knowledge of Self and the more awake you are, the more you will recognise and embrace this truth. The purpose of Life is to live every formative experience to the utmost. This is how you were as an infant, before being exposed to the notion of guilt, or the impulse to blame, or the feeling of being shamed.*

REALISATION. *The overriding and repetitious message of this book is: Never be a prisoner of the past. The past was just a lesson, not a Life-sentence! When you have been blamed by others, or when you inflict blame on yourself and experience self-recrimination it is easy to become stuck in a 'locked down' reality about your self-worth. It is easy to start viewing Life from a victim mentality and to allow the notion of guilt to make you feel disconnected. Know that you cannot be separated from the Life-giving, Universal Source, that never judges. You are safe and you're OK! Take in every entitlement Life is providing and speak your new realisation over and over again, until it becomes your truth: "The past was just a lesson, not a Life-sentence".*

METANOIA. *Freedom of heart, spirit, mind and will is what you need to be truly alive! The more consciously aware you become, the more that happiness, joy and wisdom will light up your every choice and decision. You are now paving the way for your own personal sovereignty to emanate and make its presence fully felt. You will find you are far less prepared to settle for a victim mentality and for a false concept of truth. Take in the liberating message of the next chapter. Savour it as you remember the truth of your essence. Allow your personal sovereignty to light up your highest choices. Take full responsibility for your unique and impactful presence wherever you go, with whomever you are with, and in whatever you do.*

Personal sovereignty:
Free will and responsibility

Nature is busy creating absolutely unique individuals, whereas culture has invented a single mould to which all must conform. It is grotesque

–U.G. Krishnamurti

Being a sovereign person means remembering and realising your true essence, your own worth, your own value. Living as a sovereign person means being able to choose your own actions and reactions from *within*. When you are aware of your own sovereignty, you are never persuaded, coerced or forced to conform. You will not "fall in line with", the teaching, dictates or demands of others, over your own heart-felt choices and decisions. Freedom of heart, spirit, mind and will, can only be enjoyed when you begin to honour your own personal sovereignty above all else.

We have all been conditioned to look outside of ourselves for permission from others, rather than to act confidently from our own 'knowing'. We have also been conditioned to believe the direction given to us, rather than trust our own internal guidance system. The more we seek permission from elsewhere, the more imprisoned we become within the concepts of other people's beliefs.

Know this and become aware ...

**Every belief has a fear attached to it!
Once you enter into a belief, you are
constantly left asking yourself;
"If I don't do this, what's going to happen?"
The difference between *knowing* and *believing*
is fear. Belief comes from the outside, while
knowing comes from the inside.**

Because you have not been taught to treat your own sovereignty as sacred, you have not learned how to honour it. Instead, you have followed the beliefs of others and made them your own, even when they are the beliefs of someone else about how to live your own Life. You have been doing this, often without even being aware of it. You have been doing it from the moment an authority, other than your own, assumed a position of dominance over you. As an infant in school, you had to put your hand up to ask if you could go to the toilet. Prior to that, you certainly didn't have to seek permission from your mummy, did you? Yet from such an early stage in your childhood development, you were becoming subservient to an authority outside of yourself, even for as personal a function as the permission to relieve your bladder. From that time onward, not only did you adopt the idea that people are superior to your own needs, you also had to accept the decision they chose to make for you in that moment. The answer given to you may have been ...

"No. It's almost break time and you can go then".
Or, it could have been ...
"Yes, but make it quick".
Or it may have carried a warning, for you to further take notice of ...
"Yes, alright, but in future you must go before class begins".

Encapsulated in this one personal incident, you were instantaneously imprinted by:

• The belief that another person's judgment is the authority you accept

- The fear of what repercussions another's judgment could mean for you

- The acceptance that another person's decision, decides for you

- The recognition that another's superiority can be controlling of you

Next, comes the introduction of religion with its depictions of Heaven and Hell, punishment for wrong-doings committed on earth and, as long as you earn enough grace, *possible* redemption in the next Life. Wow! Quite an onslaught so far, and all this while you are still learning how to read and write.

Then comes your introduction to the subject of history. A very carefully selected mix of 'stories' from random periods in times past, where education systems choose to indoctrinate children with neatly packaged versions of days gone by. Inevitably, each culture only highlighting the stories of their own victories in battles and wars fought, for the freedom and greater glory of all. 'His - story' of course, is only written by the winner of wars, in case you hadn't noticed! And so we digest whatever story of 'His' that's given to us to believe.

At some stage, often while still in childhood, you may have been taken to the doctor if you were sick. In the western world, pills and medicines are the means by which medical practitioners 'cure' sickness. However, if you find six months later, or perhaps even ten years later that you are still being prescribed the same medication for the illness you originally complained of, then shouldn't you be asking ...

"Wasn't this prescription supposed to *cure* me?"

Sadly, humanity has forgotten its *knowing* and has traded its sovereignty and the wisdom of our own internal guidance system, for *believing*. Guilt ensures that we remain subservient to those who set themselves up as an authority and, not surprisingly, many individuals and institutions deliberately use guilt to manipulate and exploit a victim mentality.

Hear the call that is being made to you NOW and ... *wake up from the lie you've been living*. It is time to trust your sovereignty and act for yourself. It is time to live your own truth. Pause now and consider the many revelations and new realisations this book has already opened up to you. The more you honour your own personal sovereignty, the faster you will grow up. The more awake you are to truths that have been concealed from you, the more your inner-knowing will reveal itself to you. This is a good time to consult your own wisdom now, as you allow the imposition of guilt and shame to fall away from you.

Have you ever experienced anything *outside* of yourself?
The answer is, No.

Everything that ever happened to you and every experience,
whether you perceived it to be good or bad, right or wrong,
darkness or light, joy or sadness, happened *within* you.

Pause now and make that revelation your new realisation.

Now, ask yourself again ...
Have you ever experienced anything *outside* of yourself?
The answer again will be, No.

If you look at a child, from where do you see him/her?
From *within* you!
As you look at your partner, from where do you see him/her?
From *within* you!

So what is it that's happening *within* you? Who determines
what you see, what you hear, what you experience?
Is it somebody or something else? No.

YOU determine what you experience in Life, only you!

How you experience Life on this planet is 100% determined by you.

If you ever leave it to influences *outside* of you, just about everyone will determine your Life for you. As you well know. And, has that ever served you well? No.

These are questions the Indian yogi and mystic Sadhguru recommends we ask ourselves when we feel ready to reinstate essential truths about our sovereignty. He calls it the process of "inner engineering". Of course, not many of us have ever been taught to pause and do some necessary "inner engineering". Quite the opposite. You have become conditioned to believe, not question, and you have remained imprisoned within the concepts of those beliefs.

Know this and become aware ...

It is vital to elicit, understand, protect, and treat as sacred your own personal sovereignty, because it can radically transform your existence.

When you are aware and respectful of your own sovereignty, you are living Life as the Individuation of the Divine that you are. Living your truth, from within. You will no longer lie to yourself or have others lie to you. You will not punish others and not let anyone punish you.

As you continue to read the remaining chapters, aware of your own sovereignty, you will be starting from a place of truth. You will have more confidence to proceed, without the stranglehold of guilt keeping you so diminished. The beautiful experience of METANOIA can now unfold freely, for it is your own inner-knowing that will be your most reliable guide.

The reason this REVELATION has not been REALISED by you before, is because it is a truth which has not been taught to you before. Nor has it been demonstrated to you consistently enough, by those who were principally entrusted with the care and responsibility of bringing you through childhood and into adulthood. Nonetheless, it is yours to resurrect. Now, all you are to *allow* is the readiness to awaken from the victim mentality that has kept you fastened in guilt and for which you've felt so ashamed.

When you are living your Life as a sovereign person *you will* ...

• Love and accept your Self as the Individuation of the Divine that you are

• Embody self and mutual respect, allowing all others to be that which they are (even those who do not respect you or their own sovereignty)

• Do no harm and take 100% responsibility for your every thought, word and action

• Detach from the controlling systems of the world by becoming less dependent, more ecological, more consciously aware about the choices you make for your health and well-being

• No longer let others make you feel weak or inferior in their presence, so they can intimidate, abuse, manipulate or control

• No longer feel the necessity to carry guilt, as if it were a Lifetime sentence

You don't have to be an activist or a revolutionary to honour your personal sovereignty. You simply need to question, question, question, rather than assume that someone or some external authority holds the answers and directions for your own Life. Consult your inner-knowing and feel what resonates with your heart, spirit, mind and will. Only you, in your personal sovereignty, will know what is true for you and no one else has the right to criticise that. It is YOUR truth.

It is important from now on, that you live your Life 'in your power' and declare the grandeur of your Being. When you acknowledge someone's character, you give them their power, your essence is acknowledging their essence. When something of a person's character is taken away from them, their ego feels considerably threatened and diminished. Ultimately, of course, loss of character can only really be brought about if the notion of guilt is allowed to totally overshadow your true nature.

Remember, *you are ...*

- Inseparable from the Source of Life

- An Individuation of the Divine

- Sovereign in your Being

Your character is not the same as your personality. Personality is a learned thing, character is the unique individuality of *Who You Truly Are*. Character is your essence, you come with it; you are born with it. Personality is borrowed along with the borrowed attitudes, borrowed thoughts and borrowed beliefs you form *about* yourself. Your character is your Self and how you make present its essence, the essence of your Being. Character requires you to be in right relationship with your Self at all times. A child is born naked into the world and he or she is given clothes to wear to cover their nakedness. A child is also born in essence, character. Unfortunately, we have been conditioned to sometimes hide that too, and to our detriment. You can no longer afford to do that.

This realisation and your acceptance of its truth goes against the grain of almost every other teaching you've been bombarded with. It goes totally against all that has been keeping you in guilt, it goes against how you've been conditioned to think and act, it goes against the victim mentality you've been operating from.

Know this and become aware …

Unless you recognise that humanity has largely been scripted by the beliefs of those who control, then your Life will forever feel restricted, undeserving, unworthy, helpless and powerless.

Indoctrination has been fed to us as truths. This is an insidious thing. Children, when left on their own, have magnificent dreams and they are always expansive. However, they are easily squashed with the imposition of guilt. When you were stopped from being expansive you became easy to manage, easy to manipulate, easy to programme, easy to condition, easy to control.

People within a hierarchical system of rule have always been kept subservient. Once land owners controlled land and property while money lenders profited from people's hardship. Now, corporations dominate the banking and financial systems and religions control the belief systems. The mainstream media manipulates and directs our thinking, while governments, through politics, straddle them all. The sovereign person needs to be alert and possess the necessary conscious awareness in order to be *in* this world, but not *of* this world.

The poet Rudyard Kipling, reminds us how to accomplish that …

"I keep six honest serving men (they taught me all I knew); Their names are What and Why and When and How and Where and Who."

To honour your personal sovereignty, take the lesson of Kipling's poem fully on board. Always question …
"Is this appropriate for me?"
"Is this going to improve the quality of my Life?"
"Is there a better way, that has not yet come into my awareness?"

To be an authentic sovereign being, there is no need to be drawn into conflict. All that is necessary, is to be aware of the illusion of duality, then there is no conflict. Become independent from those external authorities which otherwise dominate your world. Be careful not to bind yourself into having to make limiting choices—black OR white, yes OR no, this OR that. Know Life will always provide this AND that. All you are to do is to allow your Self to make more expansive decisions, more expansive choices in EVERYTHING. Otherwise, as you know, other's will always be ready to make them for you.

You never need to be limited. You require more than a binary system at your disposal to make your journey through this Life. Life has far more to offer you than just this or that. The computer works OK that way, but you do not. Once you reduce your Self to just two possible options, you reduce your Life to just two outcomes and, as an Individuation of the Divine, you will realise that not one of us was ever created to remain so limited.

Remember, your conditioning began when you first put up your hand to ask the permission of the teacher to go to the toilet! When you had to wait for the definitive answer: "Yes" OR "No". Your conditioning starts there. Your illusion of duality starts there. The struggle, all these years on, to free your heart, spirit, mind and will from guilt starts there.

Know this and become aware ...

Personal sovereignty is the intrinsic authority and power to determine your own direction and destiny. If that sounds suspiciously like free will, it's because personal sovereignty and free will are the same thing!

It is also necessary to distinguish between having sovereign 'rights' and *being* a sovereign person, because they are not the same thing.

Being sovereign is knowing how to move beyond the imposition of guilt. That doesn't mean you simply give yourself the 'right' to do anything you want without regard for others; that would be psychopathic or sociopathic behaviour, lacking the necessary empathy which is central to every consciously aware sovereign being. A sovereign person will always consider the personal sovereignty of others, in fact it is the development of our own sovereignty that brings us to the realisation of oneness.

Essentially, as you embrace your own sovereignty you become more aware of your eternal connectivity with the Divine. You also heighten the importance of self and mutual respect in every interaction and in every relationship you form, further empowering you to drop the notion of guilt from your thinking and from your vocabulary altogether.

Ultimately, we can each demonstrate only as much power of sovereignty, as much self and mutual respect, and as much freedom in our lives, as we have become awakened to. The purpose of this book, which is perhaps becoming more clear to you, is to teach you *how* to reclaim the maximum amount of sovereignty required to move you from guilt and shame, through remorse, and from remorse through regret, and finally from regret to connectivity once again.

It's the experience of:

SELF-FORGIVENESS.
(REVELATION, a new discovery about your Self and about Life)

SELF-HEALING.
(REALISATION of your inseparable union with the Divine)

CONSCIOUSNESS UNFOLDING.
(METANOIA, closing the illusion of duality and restoring freedom of heart, spirit, mind, and will)

The intellectual tradition that has brainwashed every human being, and kept your own sovereignty hidden and undeveloped until now, has ensured you remained rooted in the stranglehold of guilt. You will have become frightened to demonstrate anything, other than servility, to those who have assumed importance over you. You will have been ashamed to trust and fully embrace your own powerful presence and worth.

The more you continue to let your intellect be conditioned and programmed by relationships that are controlling and manipulative, the more you will have become governed and ruled by their thinking. Rules are made to control and it's not surprising that we can all be driven to break a lot of rules as we proceed through Life. However, it is also important to be aware that each rule broken sets in motion the very stuff that control is most dependant upon. The strongest and most manipulative form of control used by those who assume power over you, is of course the insidious imposition of guilt.

The way to increase your personal sovereignty is to increase your free will, and as you increase your free will, you increase your own accountability. You will do this most effectively the more consciously aware you become. Greater awareness of your true nature, as the Individuation of the Divine that you are, will determine what actions to take and what reactions to have in any given situation. Blame and the self-recrimination of shame, will inevitably become the impulsive reactions you resort to less. The more aware of your true nature you are, the better you will discover how to interpret your impulses. You will quickly spot if they are being freely chosen by you, or whether they are simply the reactions you have been programmed and conditioned to unconsciously act out.

Beware, though. Personal sovereignty has a high price. It's called personal responsibility. As you increase your use of free will, you also increase your responsibility for your actions and reactions. Increase it enough, and you won't be able to blame your parents, your enemies, your friends, your lovers or spouse, society, fate, Satan or God or anybody else. It also goes without saying, that if a lot of people were to greatly increase their personal responsibility our society would undergo tremendous change.

In the next chapter, we will identify that which has so effectively thwarted such change. We will see more clearly what has kept humanity rooted in fear and which requires the notion of guilt to keep a victim mentality firmly in place. Once again we will see that we have been indoctrinated in the belief that one of only two possible outcomes awaits us at the end of Life ... *Heaven* OR *Hell*.

Guilt has kept us cautiously and fearfully on our toes. We trust that obedience to those who have constructed our beliefs on this earth, will in time be duly rewarded by the 'God' authority that decides our fate in the next world!

REVELATION. *Never be afraid to question the true motivations and honesty of any information being presented to you. Always see beyond fear mongering. Stay aware and determine what your inner truths are at every step of the way. Life is inviting you right now, to take the leap of consciousness and to undergo tremendous change for yourself. It is to begin to live more from love than from fear.*

REALISATION. *Be aware of your sovereignty. Make conscious decisions based on sound judgment and wisdom, instead of being dependent on dogmatic opinions and delusions. Take 100% responsibility to live Life with a free heart, a free spirit, a free mind and a free will. It is time to drop the illusion of guilt and shame from your consciousness altogether.*

METANOIA. *Confidently speak from your inner-knowing, make your sovereign presence more noticeably present. As you meet Life's various challenges, when circumstances and incidents stir fears and uncertainty within you, know that it is the ego and not your Being, which is afraid. The ego is of very limited assistance to you. It belongs to your bodily existence alone. It is nothing more than an accumulation of ideas; thoughts and associated feelings about things. You have an ego, but you are not the ego. The ego will die. Life does not. Take back your power and dissolve whatever trace of guilt the ego presents. Deeply, lovingly, unconditionally accept your personal sovereignty.*

Religion and Sin, Heaven and Hell: A masterful guilt trip

Guilt was never a rational thing, it distorts all the faculties of the human mind, it perverts them, it leads a man no longer in the free use of his reason, it puts him into confusion.

–Edmund Burke

There is an interesting story about an Eskimo hunter who asked the local missionary priest, "If I did not know about God and sin, would I go to Hell?" "No", said the priest, "not if you did not know." "Then why," asked the Eskimo earnestly, "did you tell me?"

Amusing as that little story is, it contains a profound truth and an important revelation. Perhaps you will choose to make its revelation one of your new realisations.

At this point in the book, you may well be wondering how different your own Life would be, had you been more ready to question things you were taught to believe. Maybe you are now beginning to see that the imposition of guilt and all the misery and anguish that came with it, has stemmed from beliefs you've long held but not ever stopped to question.

Know this and become aware ...

Your investment in the belief that you were powerless and in need of a rescuer has been hugely detrimental and damaging. Once you become more consciously aware of that, you begin to grow, you begin to expand, you begin to live more freely.

Once guilt was created in your mind, everything that had freedom and ease about it, everything that was once unbridled, everything that naturally displayed your character, your essence, your sovereignty, was repressed. All that was once adventurous became less outgoing. You became uncertain. With the idea of guilt, your potential became stifled, hidden from you and hidden from others. Inevitably, you traded independency: a free heart, spirit, mind and will for dependency: reliance on that which you believed would be 'protective' of you. Like many, you may have looked toward a saviour, a messiah, a deity, a power 'higher' than your own Self as your rescuer. Not surprisingly, there has never existed any shortage of rescuers ready to take you under their wing. They are more commonly known as religions.

The years between 600 B.C. and 600 A.D. (after Christ) saw the beginning of many of the world's major religions. This period saw the flowering of Zoroastrianism and Judaism, together with the births and lives of the Buddha, Confucius, Lao Tzu, Jesus Christ, and Mohammed. You might say, things have never been quite the same since!

Over time, across every pocket of the planet, organised religions have continued to proLiferate, dividing into churches, denominations, congregations, religious bodies, faith groups, tribes, cultures, and movements. Astonishingly, there are some 4,300 world religions compared with 6,800 living languages spoken somewhere in the world and a massive 75 percent of the world's population practices one of the five most influential religions, either Buddhism, Hinduism, Islam, Judaism or Christianity.

The world's biggest religion is Christianity, with a third of humanity as its followers. Other religions make up the remaining percentage; Sikhism, Chinese traditional religion, Spiritism, Baha'i, Jainism, Shinto, Can Dai, Tenrikyo, Unitarian-Universalism, Juche, Neo Paganism, African traditional and Diaspora, and Primal-indigenous.

Of the five 'major' religions, Judaism, Christianity and Islam are the three main surviving monotheistic religions. These are all 'revealed' religions, where followers believe that 'God' spoke directly to the prophets and that those conversations were infallibly recorded in their holy books. They all believe that their interpretation of 'God' is the surest route to salvation, and preach of a struggle between good and evil both in this Life and on the spiritual plane. Despite the hostility that has often erupted among and between these belief systems, they all agree on the same universal 'God', share common prophets and respect the same Old Testament Bible.

What religions have brought to humankind is something else! Their power claims, made in the name of 'God', have given them enormous license to control. How they've pulled it off is really quite ingenious, though not without being disingenuous to us all. Not only have religions mastered their own ways of infusing layer upon layer of guilt in their believers, but they have also conjured up their own unique remedy for it. You might say, religions have perfected the art of instilling both the 'problem' and the 'solution' all in one package. Religions have called mistakes and errors 'sins', then provided the confessional as the ultimate rescue remedy; pardon and absolution from all past 'sins' committed. How manipulative is that?

There's a further catch too, written in the small print of Christian religions, that which is called 'original sin', or 'inherited sin'. Original sin is the doctrine which teaches that our otherwise perfect state of Being - totally inseparable from the Source of Life - was forever left tainted by the very first sin committed. This myth, which has been kept alive as if it were fact, stems from the biblical narrative of Adam and Eve (later to become the basis of the disastrous Christian doctrine of original sin). It is a story which ensured that the illusion of duality was well and truly cemented in the human psyche.

The narrative describes Adam and Eve as the first man and woman, the ancestors of all humans. It depicts them basking in the Garden of Eden enjoying their completeness and sovereignty, as stewards over all creation. According to the text, however (Genesis. 2:5-3:24 of the Old Testament Bible), boundaries were set in this paradise. The first human family were given access to every single thing present in the garden save one; the tree of knowledge of 'good' and 'evil'. It stood in the centre of the garden and the fruit of this tree was "the forbidden fruit". The human creatures were not to eat of the fruit of this tree, for it was said that if they ate, their eyes would be opened and they would know 'good' from 'evil'. Of course, fruit that is forbidden holds tremendous appeal for the human mind and after listening to the voice of temptation incarnate in a wily serpent, Adam and Eve disregarded the prohibition and ate of the fruit of the off-limits tree. 'God' had been disobeyed. The perfection of creation had been ruined. Human Life had fallen into 'sin'.

According to the biblical story ... the effects of this fall were immediate and permanent. The eyes of Adam and Eve were opened. They saw themselves separated from 'God'. They felt shame and guilt. They covered their nakedness with fig leaf aprons. When 'God' came to walk with Adam and Eve that evening, they now perceived this 'God' not as their creator, the Source of Life, but as their judge - the elicitor of their guilt - and so they hid. Communion with the Divine, was broken.

When 'God' found these creatures hiding in the bushes, the reality of the fall became obvious. A divine enquiry commenced, which revealed the human pattern of making excuses and blaming others. Human beings in their fallenness could not even accept responsibility for their own actions. Adam blamed Eve and God. Eve, he said, had been the cause of his downfall, but 'God' had been the fashioner of Eve. In turn, Eve blamed the serpent. The ego was now in the driving seat.

Punishment quickly ensued and, as the story asserted, Life from then on, would be a struggle. We can all, of course, testify to the last bit, but can you now see *how* we have been made to feel so unworthy, incomplete and dependent? Can you now see *how* we've been convinced that Life even needs to be a struggle? Can you see *how* we've been frightened into accepting that Life is nothing other than an endless task; always having to prove ourselves to be worthy enough of it?

This was a fascinating myth and, even more fascinating, is the fact that for most of Christian history it has been treated quite literally! It has been used to teach a message of fear and it has kept us in ignorance of our true nature. It has totally disempowered humanity and created a victim mentality. It feeds a belief in our 'incompleteness' and has formed a separatist tradition. We have been brainwashed into believing that we are a population of 'sinners' and miserable wretches, begging for mercy. Not only is the lie of original sin unacceptable but it is based on assumptions and false information. You are not and never can you be separated from your Source.

Know this and become aware ...

**Original sin is a lie against humanity.
It's time to identify it as the lie that it is, and to
realise that it has been used to keep you locked in
the falsehood of duality. No longer can you remain
ignorant of your true nature. It is time to stop being
so gullible and subservient to the power claims of any
authority which keeps you in a victim mentality.
There is no such thing as original sin.**

There's more to this lie though than we've touched on so far, and here comes the real kicker ...

It's the next part of the Adam and Eve narrative that religion - Christianity in particular - has made as the central foundation for its heavy artillery of fear mongering doctrines, and upon which it has assumed authority and control. Because of this 'sin' on the part of the first human beings, all human Life thereafter, it was asserted, would be born in 'sin' and would suffer death, the ultimate consequence of 'sin'. From this act of 'disobedience', as the teaching of Christianity promulgated, all Life stood in need of redemption. Every human being was in need of salvation, as a result of Adam and Eve's 'fall'. A rescuer would be required, a saviour from our 'sins'. Dependency, neediness, unworthiness and guilt, became central to the religious story and the principle tenet of Christian teaching. Not only was the sense of guilt embedded in our psyche, as was the perceived need to be rescued from our 'sin', but each separate religious institution asserted that it alone held the power and authority to provide us with the only true saviour and the only true pathway to 'Heaven'.

• In Judaism these claims are written into the Torah in the Ten Commandments: "I am the Lord your God who brought you out of the land of Egypt, out of the house of bondage. You shall have no other gods before me" (Exodus. 20:2). The punishment described in the law for worshipping a God other than Yahweh is death (Deuteronomy. 8:19).

• In Islam this exclusive claim is asserted in the sacred Muslim chant: "There is but one God [Allah] and Mohammed is his prophet."

• In Christianity their claims have most often been attached to the Fourth Gospel, in the New Testament of the Bible, where Jesus is quoted as having said, "I am the way, and the truth and the Life, no one comes to the Father but by me." (John 14:6). This mentality is particularly present in the assertion made by the more Catholic side of Christianity with its power claim, "There is no salvation outside the church."

The more humanity has evolved and the more conscious we have become, the more religious establishments have had to do some major surgery on their various power claims. The first line of defence was to move from a literal Adam and Eve to a symbolic Adam and Eve, and from a literary story of Life in the Garden of Eden to a symbolic story of human expulsion from the perfection that 'God' had intended for us in creation. However, despite attempts made to tinker with the wording of its doctrinal content over the centuries, such efforts have not removed the lie it was all founded upon. The Christian belief that the universal human condition is in perpetual need of redemption from 'sin' remains absolutely unaltered and intact.

Because religious domination has largely gone unchallenged and because you have not questioned it sufficiently - or realised how impactful it has been on humanity - it will be one of the reasons why your own struggle with guilt has become so unnaturally natural to you! In other words, you may never have felt comfortable with your own sense of guilt, but you've not ever given yourself the permission to call it to a halt. You never knew you had that authority, and therefore never thought to examine the extent to which guilt has affected *every* aspect of your Life.

Surprisingly, whether you think yourself to be religious minded or not, you won't have been able to escape its domineering influence. The self proclaimed 'nonreligious' people in the world make up some 1.1 billion of the populace, most often describing themselves as Secular, Agnostic or Atheist. Reportedly, atheism is said to be the fastest growing trend amongst those who do not profess belief in 'God' or have affiliation to any religious grouping. Many people of our current generation are simply not able to make sense of, or identify with the 'God' of judgment and retribution presented by the religions. That's not to say that spiritual development, countenance and direction is no longer being sought after, but It is fair to say that it is not being sufficiently inspired or nurtured by our existing organised religions. What is clear though, is that if the nonreligious populace were to share anything at all in common with the religious populace, it would most likely be .... yes, you've guessed it, ... subservience and G-U-I-L-T.

While the nonreligious may not often display guilt quite so overtly as religious people are conditioned to do, it's there, nonetheless. Guilt has been deeply embedded in us all and by a variety of means, not least through the language of political theology. For a millennia it has been the only language humans thought they had available to them and today countless millions still pursue the age-old quest to bring the whole of human Life under 'God's' authority. It has been enough to keep the illusion of separateness (duality) unquestioned, unchallenged and unchanged. It has also successfully kept humanity subservient to the power claims of those who have used it to control.

For example ...

Every American citizen has been imprinted by the religious version of 'God', whether they are consciously aware of it or not, whether they are staunch believers or ardently atheistic. The use of the phrase *"In God We Trust"* is imprinted on U.S. currency and has been recognised as a national motto. The phrase *"under God"* was also added to the Pledge of Allegiance as part of the 'cultural war' on godless communism. Today it reads: *"I pledge allegiance to the flag of the United States of America, and to the republic for which it stands, one nation under God, indivisible, with liberty and justice for all."*

Similarly, in the United Kingdom, the phrase *"God Save the Queen"* (alternatively *"God save the King"*, depending on the gender of the reigning monarch) is the national or royal anthem in the UK. It is also the anthem in a number of Commonwealth realms, their territories, and the British Crown Dependencies. We have all learned to say to the one in whom the power to judge was vested *"Your Honour"*, and to our kings, emperors, and our dictators; *"Your Majesty"*, *"Your Excellency"*, *"Your Lordship"*. To those who were presumed to speak for or represent 'God', we are expected to address them with grandiose titles such as *"Your Grace"*, *"Your Holiness"*, *"Holy Father"*.

According to the Courts and Tribunals Judiciary, when judges are sworn in, they take an oath by *Almighty God*. But Muslims may say: "I swear by Allah." Hindus may say: "I swear by Gita," a reference to a holy book. Sikhs may say: "I swear by Guru Nanak," the founder of Sikhism. Also in the law courts, no person religious or otherwise, can be excused from having to swear on oath when giving witness. In most countries, the practise is to "*swear by Almighty God [to tell] the truth, the whole truth, and nothing but the truth.*" Witnesses and defendants are requested to hold a holy book (usually the Bible) as they swear their oath. In recent times, motions have been made to scrap the oath, but to no avail. Those belonging to other faiths are permitted to hold other holy books—Muslims can hold the Koran, Jews can place their hand on the Old Testament, but no one is exempt from the procedure. It is law. "*Under God*" judgment is made and no other right is ours.

The 'God' our religions have taught us to be fearful of, is the 'God' embedded in the human psyche. It is the 'God' who watches our every move and notes our every thought, word and deed. It is the 'God' who stands in judgment, who punishes transgressions, and from whom we cannot hide (just as in the story of Adam and Eve). It is the 'God' who decides our fate in this world and in the next. Fictitious as this version of the Divine is, the ruling bodies and power-wielding forces on earth have been quick to hijack the idea of a vengeful 'God'. It might make you wonder if our current legal deterrent and our religions would have survived so long, had they not had Heaven as the ultimate reward or Hell as the ultimate punishment.

If you have reached a stage in your Life when you have dismissed as all but meaningless the traditional content these religious institutions have imposed upon the concept of Life after death, then you will likely have no interest in a system of rewards and punishments. You will not see the purpose of Life after death to be a motivating behaviour in the here and now. Perhaps you have reached the point when you can live without any sense of Heaven as a place of reward or Hell as a place of punishment. However, for those of you who have struggled terribly with religiously imposed guilt, (scrupulosity, toxic shame, and obsessive compulsive disorder (OCD) being amongst the most painful of those struggles), it's important you step back from it and re-examine its authenticity. It is necessary to call to question all its weird and terrifying ideas about reward and punishment. It is crucial to put some of its preposterous power claims under the microscope. It is vital to review the extent to which you've felt bound by them, but never felt empowered enough to release yourself from them.

In many cultures little choice is afforded to those who wish to opt out from a religious practice, or to those who choose an alternative form of spiritual allegiance to the one they inherited from their parents. Family estrangement or disownment is all too common an experience for many who do decide to venture away from the religious allegiance expected of them. Just as in the case of someone who has been distanced because of a Lifestyle choice: sexuality; gender; choice of partner; financial choices or for generally not behaving in the way their family prefers, conversations about religious differences are often instantly shut down. In more extreme cases, verbal and physical abuse, death threats and financial blackmail can also result among some religious families whose daughters or sons choose to leave the faith. Religions have often left people terribly confused, riddled with guilt and filled with shame.

We could pick out any religion to highlight the ways it has implemented its control methods in the name of 'God' and how it has consistently got things so appallingly messed up, but the Roman Catholic Church might be a good starting place. Many would argue that Catholicism and religiously imposed guilt are but two sides of the same coin, so let's find out shall we?

Just as a word of warning, if you're unfamiliar with Catholic doctrine, you may find some of the following content to be disturbing. So fasten your seat belts, put on your hard hat and away we go ...

The Roman Catholic Church has laid out clearly defined steps for its believers to follow, if they wish to be *cleansed* from 'sin'. Here are the requirements if a Catholic is to gain entry into Heaven and avoid any possibility of Hell's eternal damnation:

- Accept that Christ's death on the cross atoned for the original sin of Adam and Eve's disobedience and fall

- Accept that only 'God's' grace can *cure* this 'sin'

- Regularly and sincerely confess your own 'sins' and ask for forgiveness

- Be baptised (most baptisms take place in early infancy to avoid the risk of a child dying before being released from original sin)

Now let's see what all that involves ...

The theory of 'original sin' was first formulated by the 4th century Christian theologian and philosopher Augustine of Hippo. Augustine believed that 'sin' was transferred from generation to generation through the sexual act that leads to conception. Sexual desire was bad, he taught, because it could totally overwhelm those caught up in it, depriving them of self-control and rational thought. The most significant feature of sex, said Augustine, was the "involuntariness" of the male erection (*sometimes absent when you want it; sometimes present when you don't*). Painfully misogynistic, Augustine decided that because male "nature" was uncontrollable, it was women who had to be constrained!

Augustine, in fact, became the great instigator of guilt, remaining blind to the price that others had to pay for his righteousness. He supposed that there was an inherent pollution and sinfulness in sexual union, the means by which 'sin' entered the world. For Augustine, a woman's pains in childbirth were in themselves clear evidence of the sinfulness of the original act. He thought that it was just as bad and uncontrolled in a marriage as it was in non-marital sex, but that an excuse could be made for it within marriage because its purpose was to produce legitimate children. This 'bad' element in sex, according to Augustine, transmits both humanity's guilt for Adam's 'crime' and the 'sickness' or 'defect' that gives human beings a sinful nature.

"... whenever it comes to the actual process of generation, the very embrace which is lawful and honourable cannot be effected without the ardour of lust .... [This lust] is the daughter of sin, as it were; and whenever it yields assent to the commission of shameful deeds, it becomes also the mother of many sins. Now from this concupiscence whatever comes into being by natural birth is bound by original sin..."

–Augustine [De bono coniugali]

Later, in the 16th century, even more disastrous for us all, Augustine's dark and twisted view of sex and human nature was given the official stamp of approval by the Church. It became one of its central doctrinal teachings and we've been struggling with the fallout ever since! Thanks to Augustine and the Church, guilt and the feeling of being ashamed over the most natural of human proclivities was inculcated into generation after generation of humanity. It has become an irrational and morbid guilt which is no less present among 'believers' in the twenty first century as it was in the second or third century. It also led to the Church becoming sex obsessed and devising a remarkable catalogue of 'sins' along with penances suitably served for each 'offence' committed ...

ORIGINAL AND ACTUAL SIN

• Original: *The act of disobedience by Adam. Inherited at conception but, for the lucky ones, remitted in baptism.*

• Actual: *A voluntary act of individual will.*

MORTAL AND VENIAL SIN

• Mortal: *Intrinsically, always and absolutely evil, e.g. blasphemy.*
• Venial: *Pardonable, excusable (can even include killing!).*

CAPITAL, CARDINAL AND GRAVE SIN (DEADLY SIN)

• Transgressions fatal to spiritual progress: pride, envy, lust, anger, greed and sloth (later replaced by the rather vague 'sin" of sadness in the 17th Century).

FORMAL AND MATERIAL SIN

• Formal Sin: *When someone intentionally helps another person carry out a 'sinful' act.*

• Material Sin: *When a person's actions unintentionally help another person do something wrong.*

INTERNAL SIN (THOUGHT CRIME)

• Delectatio Morosa: *The pleasure taken in a sinful thought or imagination even without desiring it.*

• Gaudium: *Dwelling with complacency on sins already committed.*

• Desiderium: *The desire for what is sinful.*

HABITUAL SIN (IN A STATE OF SIN UNTIL RESTORED BY PENANCE)

• Sin of commission: *A positive act contrary to some prohibitory precept.*

• Sin of omission: *Failure to do what is commanded.*

In Augustine's judgment – and subsequently that of the Church – sexual desire and gratification ("lust") had to be controlled, limited and confined. Libido was stigmatised as a 'sin', detracting us from 'God'. In contrast, celibacy, chastity and virginity were lauded as being far closer to the perfection of 'God' and were to be the choices of preference. Centuries of misery – sexual and psychological – were the consequence as millions became celibates or fought their own nature.

For Augustine, 'proper' love exercises a denial of selfish pleasure and the subjugation of corporeal desire to 'God'. The only way to avoid evil caused by sexual intercourse is to take the 'better' way and abstain from marriage. Since such precepts severely threatened the continuance of the human race, passionless, matrimonial intercourse *solely for the procreation of children* remained permissible, though even this was a *venial* 'sin'. Premarital and extramarital sex clearly were 'sins', as was sex during pregnancy or after childbearing age. Even the harmless release of masturbation became a grave sin, the crime of 'Onanism'. In confession, the 'sin' of masturbation to be absolved, is not only from the perceived 'waste' of seed by the male, but for whatever pleasure was taken from the act by either male or female! What corrupt way of thinking is that? And there is more, much more ...

As a result of Adam's transgression, Augustine arrived at the conclusion that all people are *sinners from birth*. This even applied to people who hadn't committed any 'sins', like newborn babies, if they died before their souls were 'cleaned' by baptism. He couldn't guarantee that everyone who was baptised would be saved from damnation, merely that those who weren't baptised would go to Hell! It can only be supposed from such bizarre thinking, that babies born before Christ—were just too unfortunate to have been born at the wrong time!

> *"Unconscious infants dying without baptism are damned by virtue of their inherited guilt."*

Augustine [*Newman, Manual of Church History*, Vol. I, p. 366].

After deliberating on 'sin' at synods in Rome and Carthage (251/252 AD), the Church decided that *no one* could avoid *venial* 'sin', and therefore all needed the intercession of the Church. But it also ruled that *"all sins were forgivable with sufficient penance"*, and here, potentially, was a vast business in the making, because Augustine made clear that it was only the Catholic hierarchy that held the right to forgive and the power to absolve from 'sin'.

No individual could remove 'sin' by himself or herself no matter how 'righteous' they might be. Only within the embrace of *Holy Mother Church* could a person be 'saved'. New born babes were now 'sinners' like the rest of us. There was no escape.

Common *venial sins* could be remitted by prayer, confession to the clergy, contrition, fervent communion, and other 'pious works', all of which required frequent attendance at Church and appropriate service or recompense to the officiating clergy.

The saintly Augustine had also provided the dubious theology of *Purgatory*, a holding pen where even compliant Christians would find themselves after death, a place where "fire might wash them free of sin".

More serious *mortal sins* required even greater sacrifice on the part of the sinner. According to the demented theology, 'sin' must be atoned for either in this world or in the world to come. Punishment in the future Life would be proportionate to the "sin committed" in this Life but would also last forever.

You've got to admit that's all a tad harsh from a 'God' of love and goodness, don't you think?

In the future Life, warned the Church, the penalty for 'sin' would be the 'pain of loss' – that is, "privation of the beatific vision of God", meaning eternal separation from our Source. Torment in Hell awaited the 'sinner'. As the centuries progressed, that Christian portrayal of 'Hell' was depicted in art, preached from pulpits, and even eluded to by judges in law courts on pronouncing judgment as an even nastier place. Not surprisingly, we have all gradually accepted, without question, that a system of reward and punishment carried out in the world, must also be essential to Life after death!

With a blend of 'eternal bliss' (Heaven) on the one hand and a 'satanic pit' (Hell) on the other, the Church has mercilessly exploited the fears, credulity and hopes of humanity. Time has not noticeably softened the rapacity of its doctrines and guilt is still deeply interwoven into every aspect of its teaching. The image of the cross and the bleeding figure of Christ, said to have "died to save us from our sins", adorns every church building. The Church, knowing how impressionable the unconscious mind is, has fully exploited its penetrative use of symbolism. Its smells, bells and other forms of tintinnabulary bombard every one of the senses, effectively evoking in its believers a deep spiritual, psychological and emotional attachment. Loyalty, dedication and unquestioning commitment are the essential prerequisites for each believer.

Got the picture? Had enough horror stories? Amazing what 'blind faith' can have us consenting to, isn't it? Those of you of other religious faiths would do well to revisit your own practices and see if you can identify some equally bizarre requirements you've not stopped to question.

It is plain to see that those wielding such authority in the Catholic Church have been, and still are, those most neurotic about all matters sexual. It has taken something Jesus Christ hardly ever talked about and turned it into a 'sin'; a control mechanism that looks increasingly pathetic as humanity evolves.This is not an acceptable relationship for anyone to have with the Divine. From celibacy to abortion, from contraception to homosexuality, people's private sexual decisions seem to be the domain over which the Church likes to exercise maximum possible control. It has brought about a guilt-trip that became present at Sunday worship every week and which fills its prayers and services with incessant pleas for mercy from 'God'. Followers are taught to feel guilty. Begging for mercy is totally natural to the Catholic.

Being told that we are a population of 'sinners' does not help anyone, nor is it the Christ message. Humans do not need to be 'saved from sin'. Jesus Christ did not die for our sins. He says something quite different about his purpose. He says, "I have come that you might have Life." Not that I might save you from your terrible, evil selves, but that you might have Life and you might have it abundantly. That's quite a difference. That's a difference in focus, that's a difference in meaning. The unadulterated Christ message is about expanded Life, heightened consciousness and achieving an awakened humanity. It is about breaking through human barriers. It is about empowering humankind to push beyond our limits. It is about learning to reach our full human potential. Guilt finds itself redundant, when the Christ message is fully embraced and more truly practised.

Religions have used fear, and guilt in particular, as the most threatening tool in their arsenal, with promises of Heaven if we get things 'right' or eternity in the everlasting fires of Hell if we don't! Each faith has persisted with the claim that no road, other than their own, leads to salvation. It's a barbaric theology.

Know this and become aware ...

The *truth* about Heaven, Hell and Purgatory, is that they are *lies*.

People laugh and joke about burning in Hell and draw cartoons about it but almost no one can take it seriously. Believing in Hell doesn't promote righteous living but an unhealthy fear for those brainwashed to believe it is true. It is especially cruel to inflict this terror on innocent children and the uneducated and susceptible. It is hard to imagine how many lives have been ruined or devoid of joy because of all the fire and brimstone hurled at them.

Humanity is evolving and, as we become more consciously aware, many things once unquestioned are now being understood so very differently. Life does not end. You are Life and Life is You. We are eternally connected to the Divine, to the Source that is sourcing *everything*. Only the ego dies. It's dispensed with once we shed our physical form. Only the accumulated data your mind has conjured up *about* Life, *about* death, *about* fear, *about* success, *about* relationships, *about* money, *about* religion, *about* shame, *about* guilt, *about* whatever else has caused you so much confusion, pain, and suffering .... falls away, dies. It was all just made up anyway, and what you did not make up, others had made up for you. The ego identity you've created *about* yourself is finite, it's relatively short lived. You are infinite. You are an Individuation of the Divine, the Divine is sacred, and the sacred is indestructible.

If you have been racked by religiously imposed guilt, but still want to enjoy whatever else you believe can be salvaged from your chosen creed, then expand your awareness. English novelist George Orwell, best known for his books 'Animal Farm', 'Nineteen Eighty-Four' and 'Road to Wigan Pier' sums it all up in one neat sentence, *"One cannot really be Catholic and grown up"*. Arguably, the same criticism could equally be levelled at all religions. Realise that humans need to be taught how to grow as a people, how to evolve. We need to be reminded of our true nature. We need to be taught how to love and accept one another, despite our differences. We need to develop our personal sovereignty. We need to take 100% responsibility for our Life and to live it to the full. There is no room for the power claims and guilt inducing 'conditions' our organised religions have always depended upon. That's the only basis on which religions can live in the twenty first century and far beyond, but not otherwise. Each religious authority, despite the fear mongering tactics they've chosen to deploy, also *know* this to be true. They've just forgotten to remember it ...

CHRISTIANITY. *A new command I give you: Love one another. As I have loved you, so you must love one another. By this everyone will know that you are my disciples, if you love one another.* John 13:34-35

BUDDHISM. *Hurt not others in ways that you yourself would find harmful.* Udan-Varga, 5,18

ISLAM. *No one of you is a believer until he desires for his brother that which he desires for himself.*
Sunnah

JUDAISM. *Do not do to your fellow men, what is hateful to you. That is the entire Law; all the rest is commentary.*
Talmud, Shabbat, 31A

CONFUCIANISM. *Surely it is the maxim of loving-kindness: Do not unto others that you would not have them do unto you.*
Analects, 15.23

TAOISM. *Regard your neighbour's gain as your own gain, and your neighbour's loss as your own loss.*
T'ai Shang Kan Ying Pien

JAINISM. *In happiness and suffering, in joy and grief, regard all creatures as you would regard your own self.*
Yoga-Sasta

REVELATION. *Guilt, so commonly used in the form of blame by our society to manipulate and punish, manifests itself in a variety of expressions, such as remorse, self-recrimination, addiction, masochism, and the whole gamut of symptoms of victimhood. Unconscious guilt results in psychosomatic disease, accident proneness and social behaviours. Guilt domination results in pre-occupation with 'sin', an unforgiving emotional attitude frequently exploited by religious demagogues who use it for coercion and control. Obsessed with punishment, they are most often either acting out their own guilt or projecting it onto others.*

REALISATION. *The Freedom you crave, is the freedom to make mistakes, as many mistakes as it may take and to not feel unworthy or undeserving because of them. Mistakes are the natural, impersonal consequence of learning and development. They are unavoidable. Guilt is the consequence of the memory of regretted past actions, whether it occurred 5 minutes ago or 50 years ago. The past cannot be re-written, but it can be re-contextualised. Once it is, the past can immediately become an invaluable source of constructive learning. It is how to become more consciously aware. It is how to be free.*

METANOIA. *The literal, absolute definition of the word 'sin' is 'error', and although religions with their own elaborations have turned the meaning into something more grotesque and have ranked 'errors' according to alleged degrees of seriousness and culpability, there is just one single recurrent 'sin' ... to remain unconscious of our mistakes! As you grow in consciousness, you are able to look back and realise when you were behaving in an unconscious way. As soon as you do that, you have moved on. Whatever may have seemed like a good idea at the time was acted upon at that time but actually is no more; they are not the same. Guilt results from making them the same, equating your present self that 'is' with the former self that 'was'. The key to self-forgiveness, is not to forgive at all, but to understand!*

CHAPTER SEVEN

The most important decision to make: <u>What</u> you believe

There are two ways to be fooled. One is to believe what isn't true; the other is to refuse to believe what is true.

– Søren Kierkegaard

As we have seen, the majority of today's believers, and you may or may not be amongst them, will have simply subscribed to the religion of the culture in which they were raised, trusting parents to have made the best decision for them. While all religions contain much that may appeal, as well as many things that are thought to be true and noble, they each demand 'blind faith' and unquestioning trust. It is a demand that leaves no room at all for the nurturing and development of our personal sovereignty, not when it instils the belief that it's possible for us to get Life 'wrong'.

It is time religious ignorance was exposed. The word 'belief' is used over and over again, emphasising that you're either in or out of a particular idealogical system. That is nothing other than a form of bullying mind-control. These authorities are not the only voice for Christ, or Mohammad, or Yahweh. They are not the only voice for truth. They are not the only voice for you. Their negativity cannot determine what truth is. The punishing 'God' of the Bible is replicated in the punishing parent, the punishing authority figure and the punishing nation. And so ... violence is thought by the ego/mind to be redemptive, war is declared to be justified, and bloodshed as the way to salvation. It all fits together so tightly, so neatly and it justifies the most destructive and demeaning of human emotions.

It is the *idea* of 'God' as something *other* and separate from you, that has been inaccurate and which is the very root of humanity's confusion. The 'problem' created by religious thinking forms the illusion of duality: a way of looking at Life which sees that everyone is separate from everything else. Once that illusion is fed to the ego/mind it creates within each of us a feeling of *aloneness*. It is in that feeling where guilt and shame can be overwhelming and it is also in that feeling when it becomes all too easy to fall prey to victim mentality. We begin to think of ourselves as unloved or unlovable. We may even think of ourselves as failures.

Know this and become aware ...

There is no Higher Power taking score of any kind and if you will stop taking score of yourself so much, you will feel a whole lot better. As you feel a whole lot better, you will feel how much more easily Life can flow through you, and without restriction.

Most of humanity is, as yet, unconscious, unaware, unenlightened. Our religions reside in that unconscious and un-evolved state, relying heavily on reward and punishment as the basis for their moralising. Ancient and deeply ingrained beliefs, still unquestioned, block us from accepting the otherwise obvious and irrefutable logic that we are a part of all that exists, inseparable from the Divine. As a result, we have readily believed what isn't true and been frightened, reluctant or resistant to believe what is true. Because we have not been given free reign to question, or been shown how to evolve, it is not surprising that most of humanity has not even recognised the damage that is done, the confusion that is felt, the suffering caused or the conflict we endure.

Unless we do grow in consciousness we will still enter into war and we will still rely on fear and punishment as the means to correct and direct our children. We will still blame and still think it necessary to hold onto shame or make others feel ashamed. This is also why we make such a big thing of the need to be forgiven and why we think it so difficult to be forgiving of others or even of ourselves. We have frightened ourselves by believing we are unsafe. Insecurity is our greatest fear and, as a result, the need for protection has become our main pre-occupation. You were born into a world which is driven by an addictive quest for dominance and the need to control. As you entered the world, your own struggle for power also began, and your own 'control dramas'[1] soon formed your ego identity. Your instinct to survive was instantly 'switched on', accompanied by the psychological and spiritual needs for security, intimacy, financial well-being, a sense of belonging, recognition and control over your Life.

As a child, you were dependant on adult caretakers for your survival and you will have quickly developed very specific ways to take up your place within your family system and don the role you assumed. Getting enough love to feel secure and enough recognition will have been crucial to your development. It will have been *how* you formed an ego identity; how you formed your perception of reality; and how you formed the various dramas you felt compelled to act out, as you vied for attention. It will also have been how you formed your beliefs, your thoughts, your behaviours and how you are still forming your Life situations and experiences today; beneficially or detrimentally.

Some of you will have received sufficient love, affirmation and validation. Some of you will not. Some of you will have felt it necessary to adopt a victim mentality, in the hope others would see it as their duty to feel sorry for you. Some of you will have thought it more necessary to intimidate others, in order to ensure you always held centre stage. Some

---

1   James Redfield and Carol Adrienne provide a comprehensive description of the 'control dramas' in their 'Experiential Guide' - a companion book to the well known novel The Celestine Prophesy. Bantam (1995).

of you may have discovered that cross questioning others and making them feel 'wrong' and constantly answerable to your interrogation methods was the way by which you felt more dominant and in control. Alternatively, you may have adopted an aloof mode, believing that if you remained unavailable, detached, or even a little mysterious or different from others, it would often avoid being pinned down by commitments. This will have been the way you prevented others from imposing their choices and decisions over your own will. No matter which 'drama' you felt was so vital to act out, know it was driven by the innate fear that you might not survive without it. Each and every one of us discovered our own ways of making sense out of the nonsense of this world when we first encountered it. We have all been led to believe that Life needs to be a struggle and, on entering that perceived struggle, we have utilised our own survival methods.

In the first few months of your Life, like all new born babies, you will have constantly explored and experimented. It is in this formative stage of development when you decided how your experience of Life would continue to pan out. Concepts of time, space, happiness, sadness, self and non-self acceptance didn't exist for you as a baby. You had no language, so you had no thought. What you did have, however, was a rapidly evolving brain of ten billion buzzing neurons, hungry to form new connections. You began to learn, as you received the constant attention from those around you and the neurons will have started to form connections known as synapses—junctions. In fact, in the first two years of your Life some 1.8 million synapses a second will have been forged. Then, just a couple of years later, something rather drastic happened. By the time you reached two years old, nothing like as much notice and attention will have been afforded to you, as it was when you were a baby in arms. You might say, the novelty of your presence became less all-encompassing to others. As a result, over 50 percent of the initial synaptic connections made in the first two years become severed through a process known as 'synaptic pruning'. Many individual synapses may also have been completely destroyed, depending on the form of programming you were experiencing in those formative years.

By the age of four, just another two years on, a mass culling - or systematic slaughter - of those neural connections will most likely have been made, when your more instinctive desire to explore and to push out boundaries was curbed, corrected or punished by those who wanted you to behave differently.

This will have especially been the case if you experienced trauma of any kind, causing even greater destruction to your neural network; neglect, indifference, absence or detachment from parents - particularly your mother - abandonment, being left alone or with people you had not formed a close enough bond with, abuse of any kind, harshness, ridicule, bullying, excessive shouting or arguments within your environment, consistently being chastised, ignored, or any verbal, emotional, mental or physical hostility, will have combined to make you feel 'wrong'.

By this stage, you will inevitably have taken more notice of the demands and warnings of your caregivers. If you have been constantly intimidated by them, you will have been too fearful to step out of line. However, whether your introduction to this world was positive, negative, or somewhere in between, you will have started to substitute conformity for imagination, routine for creativity and the readiness to fulfil the expectations of those in authority, rather than explore the natural wonder of your own possibilities. Ultimately, only half of the neural connections made in your early months will have remained and, from what was left, you formed your reality. From there on, your conditioning and programming determined how you would see, feel, hear, touch and taste the world! The process also determined how you related as a separate person with notions such as 'I' and 'you', 'here' and 'there', all of which had been taught and reinforced by the people around you, particularly your parents. Their impact on you will have been impressionable, whether they were often or always absent from your early formative years, or constantly present throughout your childhood.

As you are reading this today, many of you will be able to recognise the magnitude of the imprint made on you in those early formative years. Some of you will at once see *where* and *why* and *how* and *when* your later struggle with guilt and shame was first introduced. You may also be aware *who* played their part in their own unconscious handling of you, and this may well have left you angered or saddened to this day. However, rather than stopping off to judge and blame - which may have been the only impulsive reaction you thought was at your disposal - pause now, and take a nice deep breath. Take in as much of Life as you wish to draw in, together with all the wisdom you require, then fully exhale. Interrupt the temptation of the ego/mind to pull you into reactionary mode and put on hold the impulse to blame, or to shame, or to go into your own shame. Instead, from your own personal sovereignty, simply become more conscious of *how* the fearful ego identity is formed in each of us. Know that there is no need to 'entertain' the ego as it pulls at you to react now. The moment you *know* there is ego involved, its pull begins to diminish. Awareness of ego is enough to diminish the ego and diminish it you must. It has already caused you quite enough frustration, pain, struggle, confusion and agitation and has burdened you enough, providing its habitual support to the needless imposition of guilt.

You are now learning to understand yourself in a whole new way. It's like learning a new language. The brain is quite literally being rewired in this very moment of new realisation, forming new synaptic connections. Old circuits are now being dismantled and more beneficial circuits are quickly being established. As you discern the difference between guilt and the impulse to shame or blame, you are becoming more conscious. You are now learning when not to go ahead with old programming. In so very many ways, consciousness is a reversal of what family, the educational system and society have force-fed us. The arising of consciousness involves a thorough *re-education*, the unlearning of much unconscious thinking and emotion and it has already been ignited in you.

Because of the *revelations* and new *realisations* you are now waking up to, you have equipped yourself with an enormous advantage over your parents, your siblings, your teachers or instructors, your guardians or caregivers. They, in all likelihood, may never have been aware, perhaps are still not aware, and may in this Life-time never become aware of their own unconscious conditioning and programming. You NOW are more consciously aware. Greater consciousness is unfolding and the instant you realise this, the opportunity for *metanoia* is made available to you. You now possess the capacity and the expanded consciousness to move beyond - transcend - your own past conditioning and all its limited programming.

Know this and become aware ...

The beliefs you formed *about* Life, *about* others and about yourself were a reproduction of the reality that was fed to you by others. Throughout your Life, you have been unconsciously playing out that perception of reality, and all its old programming, without even being aware of it. It stops the moment you wake up and begin to create your own reality.

If we continue to remain unconscious of our programming, unaware of the implications of the unquestioned and unexplored beliefs we have inherited, then we will always use guilt as a tool to control others. It has become habitual and, unless we are more conscious, we will continue to eagerly accuse, shame and affix blame, rather than look more compassionately on others.

When others are struggling to make sense of their own Life situation and their own circumstances, just as you have struggled to make sense of yours, know now that their confusion is because of their own conditioning. The imposition of guilt has kept us all unconscious of our conditioning. We simply have not been aware of the stranglehold it has had on every one of us. It has had us all behaving in a totally reactionary manner, rather than from a place of wisdom and sovereignty.

Those who projected and imprinted their limitations on you, were also unconscious of their own magnitude. You will now be aware when certain past actions and reactions of yours similarly resulted from a lack of conscious awareness.

Through awareness, transformation happens spontaneously. When you become aware of something unsettling within you - whatever it may be - never fight it! Just observe it. Detect where in your body you feel it most. For example, the stomach area holds anxiety and fear, the neck and shoulders tend to hold stress and tension, the lower back takes the strain of financial or relationship worries. The body will often give you the clue to when and why guilt is troubling you and where it is energetically residing in your physiology. The discomfort you feel will begin to subside if you allow yourself to observe it without introducing panic or judgment. There is always great understanding to be gained from your place of awareness, as the 'energy' passes through you and then dissolves.

Know this and become aware ...

Guilt and fear have not yet been matured into caution and wisdom. You are now making a different choice. You are now ready to by-pass the damaging pull of the ego/mind that has kept you feeling rooted in guilt; feeling so undeserving and so unworthy, so unconscious and so un-evolved. You have been feeling you might get Life 'wrong'. Life is inviting you to transcend unconscious thinking and behaviour and this is why this book has made its way into your hands. Treasure this realisation.

And so now to *"the most important decision"*, first posed to us in such powerful simplicity by Albert Einstein ...

"The most important decision to make, is whether we believe we live in a friendly or hostile universe."

In this powerful statement, Einstein wants us to realise that there are lasting consequences to the choice we make about this *"most important decision"* and to the belief we continue to believe. He had the wisdom and insight to realise that whatever 'belief' we hold about Life, affects every single experience we have *in* Life. He wants us to *know and become aware* that as we decide between the two, every decision we make thereafter, will fundamentally reflect this *"most important"* decision. Every thought, every behaviour, every Life situation will flow from and be directed by this fundamental core belief. Our whole programming—how we view Life and how we project the belief that underlies it, fashions the ego/mind identity and literally attracts into its wake *only* those experiences which are in alignment with it.

As we have seen, the decision to believe *what we believe* about Life is made in infancy. The *"most important decision"* of course, is initially made not by us, but for us. It is presented to us as the core belief already believed by our parents and caregivers and, accordingly, it becomes the belief that is then believed by ourselves. It is rarely revisited by us as the years go by and it will be running on automatic pilot at the back of your mind right now, without you even being aware of it. It is your programming. Nothing will have happened in your Life that has not been shaped and conditioned by this one single belief.

Today, you are being given the opportunity to decide for yourself <u>what</u> you *truly* believe. Courtesy of Albert Einstein, the enormous significance of the choice made for you when you were an infant, is being laid out before you all these years on. You now have the chance to choose again.

Choice is the greatest power you have, even more than love. After all, first you have to make the choice to be loving before you act on love. All of us were born *knowing* deep in our inner Self that every choice we make holds the potential to change our Life, yet that inner-knowing has not been fostered enough in us by others. It is precisely because that inner-knowing has not been encouraged to come forth from within you, that you have often hesitated to make choices of your own and instead let others make decisions for you. It is also why you may regularly end up angry at yourself, or at others, for how your Life turned out.

We must each take charge of our own choices, as we are always accountable for what we create. That truth is of course why we fear the power of our choices and it's why we rarely forgive ourselves for abdicating our power of choice to someone or to something else. We resent having choice taken from us too, and there is no such thing as a small choice. Every decision is a choice and every choice is a decision which reflects the value you hold about yourself.

You are always making choices and decisions, even in your sleep, and your choices continue to make decisions for you, long after you've forgotten them! One clear choice, no matter how insignificant you might think it is, can redirect the course of your Life in the blink of an eye. As Einstein has emphasised, there is no bigger choice to make than the decision to believe <u>what</u> we *truly* believe.

So ask yourself this question, and wait for the answer to come from within ...

<u>What</u> do I believe about people, about Life, and about me?

That's not the same as asking, what you *think* you believe or what you would *like* to believe, but, what do you *truly* believe about people, about Life, and about yourself?

When you retrieve the honest answer to this seemingly innocent question, new *revelations* and new *realisations* immediately become clear. Without this clarity, you remain unaware of the magnitude of your Being.

If, you've been believing in a *"hostile universe"*, a Life governed by possible reward and equally by the threat of punishment, then you can find yourself shallow-breathing your way through each day, hoping you'll get through it but never fully living it. Regrettably, most people are doing just that. They are not stopping to question <u>what</u> they believe, but consistently passing on to the next generation whatever core beliefs had been most regularly taught and demonstrated to them from infancy.

If, you've repeatedly heard that you did not deserve this or that as you were growing up, you will believe in a "hostile universe". You will think of Life as 'unsafe'. You will have developed the core belief that you were not worthy of receiving and it's a belief that will have weaved its way through every aspect of your Life, hampering you in many unexpected ways. It will most regularly have played out as a Life-time of lack, affecting your finances, your health and your relationships. Repression, suppression, addiction, depression, all result from the belief that Life is unsafe and what each of these experiences has in common with the other is G-U-I-L-T; the belief that you will feel the ultimate and shameful sense of disconnection from your Source. This is why Einstein describes the choice you make and the belief you subsequently believe *about* Life, as *the most important decision* you ever make.

If you've been believing in a *"friendly universe"*, it is unlikely that you will be reading this book! You may *like* to *think* you believe Life to be safe, but it will not have been the core belief that has been *truly* running your programming. No person struggling with guilt has *truly* believed that Life is *truly* safe. No person struggling with guilt *truly* believes that they are not here to be judged. Guilt requires the belief that we can get Life 'wrong' and the fear that we will be condemned for it. Guilt has made sure that you have consistently been on alert, always in the stress response mode of 'fight or flight' and always on the look out for someone or something that might say 'No' to you. Figuratively speaking - for anything in Life that really matters - it still feels like you are back at the age of four or five years old, still feeling the necessity to put your hand up to ask *if* you can go to the toilet! The core belief, running on auto-pilot in your unconscious mind, is that your request may receive a hostile response and that you will be refused permission, unless you can produce a deserving or worthy enough case. Such a core belief makes for a very shaky experience of Life. It completely de-rails your own personal sovereignty and provides the perfect nesting place for guilt.

Know this and become aware ...

While the world holds many challenges for us and while public opinion will generally have you believe that our environment is anything but safe, it's not surprising that Life will seem like a battle. Remember, however, that public opinion is also a core belief collectively held by those who have not yet stopped to question it. Holding onto the belief will wreak havoc in your health, for that is the power of such belief. Every cell in your body will mimic the belief of 'hostility' and similarly create its own internal war.

This book is written to remind you that your beliefs have largely been chosen for you, but they are not written in stone. A belief is only a belief, for as long as you continue to believe it. The power of your beliefs can either be Life affirming or Life denying and they are constantly making your choices and decisions for you. How you choose to view the world will ultimately define how you live your Life. It will also determine the experiences you have *in* Life. As long as you are living out the absurdity of guilt and holding onto the expectation of punishment to accompany it, then your every expectation will be fulfilled. How could it not be? The simple principle to get here is: you get what you put out!

REVELATION. *As part of your "inner engineering" consider ... How different would your Life have been, had you not allowed the forceful judgments and domineering beliefs of other influences, to supersede, negate and sometimes even adulterate your own natural experience of it? Put down the book, go within, and deeply consider that* NOW ...

REALISATION. *You attract and manifest whatever corresponds to your inner state. Either you are living as a victim in Life, or you are the beneficiary of it. Life will fulfil whichever perspective you hold and prove as true. You have become imprisoned within and hypnotised without, denying yourself access to the internal peace and external harmony that is more rightfully yours. It is so important you remember that the freedom you yearn to experience is your Soul's natural state. In order to turn your experience of Life to its more natural state you must have the willingness to question the story of condemnation that you've been repeating to yourself. Life is inviting you to relieve yourself of all that remains unquestioned, unanswered, unresolved and unforgiven within you, so you may look at it, open it up, re-evaluate its 'truth' and move beyond its constriction.*

METANOIA. *The best indicator of how more consciously aware you now are, is how you deal with Life's challenges when they arise. In the past, your perspective of reality will have been governed and directed by your unconscious programming. An already unconscious person tends to become more deeply unconscious when such challenges arise. They become fearful to choose and to decide for themselves. The more aware person will be more intensely conscious. They will know that while a similar challenge, arising in the past, may have pulled them into an even deeper sleep, any of Life's newly arising challenges are simply invitations for greater growth and expansion. Challenges arise so we may awaken to deeper wisdom.*

CHAPTER EIGHT

Morality, conscience and consciousness

We need a morality based upon love of Life, upon pleasure in growth and positive achievement, not upon repression and prohibition.

–Bertrand Russell

Becoming consciously aware of your connectivity with the Divine is not something you 'do', but rather how you 'are'. It is *being* still, *being* silent, *being* open, *being* receptive and *being* selfless. This is when you become fully aware that you are an Individuation of the Divine. In that settled state of conscious presence, you will find that there is no place for guilt. Guilt only arises when you are trying to conduct your Life through the narrow construct of the ego/mind, rather than with the guidance of your heart's intelligence. When we rely upon principles alone for our guidance and direction, we often refer to the conscience and the morality we have formed around them. And it is so easy for us to miss the fact, that even with conscience and morality, the ego/mind is still running the show.

Your conscience is not really *your* conscience. A conscience is created 'in' you, influenced, moulded and directed by the ideologies that have impacted you most: shaping your beliefs, your thoughts, your behaviours, your values, your expectations and your aspirations. From the conscience created within you, the ego/mind forms its sense of morality. If you were to have total freedom from the ideology of conscience and morality and had you been helped to become an integrated, natural Being - intelligent, understanding, and free to live your Life according to your own light - who's to say how differently 'your' conscience might be functioning today?

Guilt is part of a conscience and conscience is hugely influenced by others. If from childhood you were regularly and consistently told that "This is wrong" or "That is wrong" or "You are wrong", then the hypnosis of that belief will have deeply impacted you. You will have instinctively held back from making choices or decisions that you would otherwise have had the natural freedom to exercise for yourself. You will also have grown up with a "hostile" view of the universe and formed the unfriendly notion of duality. Guilt simply says "you're a sinner" and once you are stuck in that conscience then shame keeps you immersed in it. In fact it is possible to live your whole Life burdened by a shame conscience and it's likely that most of you reading this book will have been doing just that.

Conscience is created *inside* you from *outside* of you—formed by those who influenced you most. The majority of us have been guided to conform to an ideology that keeps order; an ideology that can be directed, governed, and which can also be controlled. We have lived in a very confused world and in a world that relies on guilt and shame to base and develop a 'code of moral conduct'. Fears of Heaven and Hell have been used to maintain conformity and have also been used to correct and shape our development.

Know this and become aware ...

Guilt is imposed by others. Shame is your possible experience of it. You can live in a shame conscience and feel very ashamed and unworthy of taking up your place in Life. Shame is an interior experience, very specific to you, tailor made by you about you and one that, over time, you can gradually submit to.

Shame can only arise because of your understanding. Your perception of shame and the way you learned to interpret it, became part of a conscience that started to form within you. It will also have housed beliefs of unworthiness and undeserving. Every situation and experience is filtered through our social/moral/religious constructs of what is right/wrong, true/false, allowed in our world/not open for consideration. Whatever we decide is relevant, based on our internal models of the polarities of true/false, right/wrong, good/bad, acceptable/not acceptable, is influenced by our perception. This is how we 'see' our world and this is how a conscience is formed.

Some people have formed a "Catholic conscience", others a "Hindu conscience", and so on, carrying into that conscience, the fundamental principles of their religious convictions. If guilt and shame have consistently been fed to us through those religious channels, a conscience will also be coloured by whatever interpretations were given to them.The moral code of conduct we then choose to live by, will similarly have its fundamental basis in those religious principles. It will also have informed our decision about how "hostile" or "friendly" we *truly* believe Life to be.

All guilt-ridden religions and cultures commonly have a negative view of Life, especially where there is a belief in a judgmental 'God': vindictive, angry, and punitive. When natural disasters happen they are commonly contextualised, and then interpreted and perceived as being punishments for our wickedness. The ego just 'loves' suffering a 'wrong'; being the martyr, being misunderstood and being the endless victim of Life's vicissitudes. While many of us may *like* to believe or *want* to believe in a "friendly" universe, the ego will more instinctively be invested in what it perceives to be challenging and "hostile". It thereby gets an enormous pay-off from sympathy, self-pity, entitlements, importance or being 'centre stage' in which the ego-self is the hero or heroine of the melodrama. The ego hoards 'slights' and injuries, nurses 'hurt feelings', and stockpiles grievances in this inner melodrama of injustice collecting.

Necessary as it is for you to be knowledgable of how the ego/mind functions, it's equally important to become aware of how 'your' conscience has been operating. It is essential for it to become benign and then it can be utilised constructively. If not decontextualised, the conscience you consult and then act upon, ends up with self-blame or an increase of guilt, shame, or the loss of self-esteem. Rather than relying on a conscience that has been influenced by so many different factors - all of which are of the ego - you will always be more reliably served, once you discover how to consult the wisdom of 'inner-knowing'. When you have confidence to trust the certainty of your heart's wisdom, you will realise that you are so much more powerful than the ego/mind, so much more comprehensively informed than by the conscience you have developed, and so much more sensitively guided than by whatever moral principles you were instructed to adhere to.

Just as a conscience is part of your consciousness, your ability to access the deep inner-knowing of your heart is also part of your consciousness. The difference between the two is that the heart's inner-knowing is independent of you, whereas the conscience you have formed is always dependent on something else for its fulfilment. It is always about something and always a reaction *to* something the mind has perceived and interpreted *through* its filter of polarities of true/false, right/wrong, good/bad, acceptable/not acceptable.

Conscience is almost entirely, if not completely, conditioned by the ego's idea of reward or punishment and so we find ourselves using terms like; "*My* conscience would never let *me* do that", or "In all conscience, *I* could not possibly agree to that", or "*I'd* love to say yes, but *my* conscience just wouldn't allow *me*", or "I don't want to be left carrying that on *my* conscience", or "It's something that weighs very heavily on *my* conscience", or "I'd do anything to keep a clear conscience". Whenever you say that something is 'on' *your* conscience, you are consulting memories from the past and retrieving data as you recall it. You then use your interpretation of a recalled memory to inform your viewpoint of the present. You may also project the same viewpoint into the future even though the circumstances of your future are, as yet, completely unknown to you.

There is no need to disregard conscience, but it is important to realise its limitation and its unreliability. Of course, so long as ego exists - and it will, as long as we have a body/mind - the perspective of the conscience you have formed will be there for you to use. However, you are not to be used by it.

Guilt and the desire to not want to feel ashamed are always interwoven. They will stir reactionary thoughts and considerable emotional disturbance within you. Often you will have tried to describe the reactions you feel by saying, "*I* have something on *my* conscience". This is because *your* conscience is a construction of the ego/mind, as is *your* way of thinking, *your* judgment, *your* reaction, *your* opinion. It is also how you view *your* possessions and whatever else you believe to be solely '*yours*'. All are of the ego. Conscience certainly acts as your internal guidance system but more usually arbitrates as your moral compass. It will feel reliable because it is familiar to you. It will also reflect the principles held by those you have valued most; parental example, religious conviction, political persuasion, cultural conditioning; moral codes of conduct as they've been presented to you and so on.

Consciousness, allows for so much more. It vastly expands your range of options and possibilities to grow and to evolve. The more consciously aware you become, the more you will be awakened to the heart's inner-knowing. It will be untainted by the ego/mind that can so easily prejudice one's conscience. From the wisdom of the heart, you can commit 'your' conscience to becoming a useful ally and teacher, rather than the sadistic self-perpetrator it's more usually prone to become.

Know this and become aware ...

**You are Consciousness unfolding; an Individuation
of the Divine; an expression of infinite, eternal
awareness having an experience in a tiny range
of frequencies that we call the 'physical world'.
The non-physical is present but not visible to the physical
plain, for its movement is at a much quicker vibration.
The physical world is nothing but a slower vibration
of energy. Even that which you call your conscience
is of limited reliability, for it also draws its data
from the same slower range of frequencies.**

At the slower vibration of energy, resides guilt and shame and blame. Also residing here, we find repression, and suppression, and depression, and addiction. 'Your' conscience is formed and informed by the various experiences you encounter and how you interpret them. The conscience you hold is also changeable. In fact it's as changeable as the wind. The same can be said of morality. What you say is 'moral' and 'good' in one situation, you may say is 'immoral' and 'bad' in another. Morality, like conscience, is at best a 'moveable feast'. Each are derivatives of the ego/mind and both work in correlation with the changing circumstances you face and at each different stage of your development. Morality shifts as circumstances shift because your values are always situational. You claim that something is 'moral' if it works in your favour, given whatever it is the ego is trying to do, or achieve, or advocate. What is dysfunctional in all of this is that you do not admit to what you are doing. Instead, you try to pretend that 'right' and 'wrong' are absolutes. The religious person will most usually declare them to be 'God's' absolutes and the ego will feel totally justified and righteous about its claim. Yet, when it suits, we all constantly excuse ourselves from those absolutes, making moral rigidity extremely flexible indeed.

Consciousness is not the same as conscience. Conscience, like everything else, is but part of consciousness. There is no Catholic consciousness, there is no Hindu consciousness. Consciousness is simply consciousness. In a word, consciousness is awareness. The more aware you are - of yourself, of your words, of your actions, of their impact, of others' emotions, of your surroundings - the more conscious you are. When you are more consciously awake and aware, you are more aligned with the universe. You begin to realise that you can experience deeper meaning in every moment.

Consciousness provides you with a much broader view and understanding of Life. When you are awake and aware, you do not depend on making absolute claims about anything at all. Judgment, opinions, and the need to be proven 'right' are no longer necessary. Life ceases to be perceived as "hostile". You reclaim and access immediate connectivity with the Divine. The inner-knowing of the heart provides your guidance and any direction you may require in each experience you encounter.

Does this mean you become totally irresponsible and care free? Quite the opposite. It is your wake up call to become 100% responsible for every decision you make. Suddenly you can see beyond the narrow lens of ego, and at last, the illusory nature of separation and duality becomes clear. You begin to realise that you are not really the 'me' that you thought you were. You realise that the idea of 'I' was just a peep-hole through which you viewed Life, and now, consciousness makes you aware of what is around it. You become aware of the peep-hole itself—the ego. You can look at it, you can feel it, you can sense it, and you know it's not you. The ego is part of you, and a conscience you've formed is also part of you; as are the beliefs, the thoughts, and the behaviours you've been behaving. All are part of you, but they are not the totality of Who You Truly Are. Consciousness is what you are.

We all have access to the heart's intelligence and we can cultivate it, so that it becomes natural to us to consult it for moment-to-moment choices and decisions in Life. Since you've not been taught how to listen to the inner-knowing of your heart's intelligence, you've depended instead on intellect alone. Intellect will hear, but it can only philosophise; it is blind, it can't see. The heart's inner-knowing is a *seer*, it has eyes. It sees truth, there is no question of thinking about it. Most people believe their intellect and their knowledge to be enough and do not draw on their heart's intelligence at all. They remain unconscious of it and totally rely upon their mind for decision-making and direction. Moral codes of conduct are of the mind. They provide principles for us to adhere to, rationalised by the intellect. Religions govern and direct totally by setting principles and, as a result, they lack sensitivity, understanding and flexibility to the changing circumstances and different needs of each individual. Life does not run on straight lines, it runs on wiggly lines and you must replace rigidity with more flexibility.

The inner-knowing of the heart helps us to increase our sensitivity and care towards others and deepens our connection with ourselves. As we slow our minds down and attune to our deeper heart feelings, our natural intuitive connection begins to flow. By listening to the signals, heart intelligence unfolds. We become more understanding of ourselves and begin to see and then respond to others with sensitivity. It's something we can access daily in order to make more effective choices and decisions. It is going to be crucial to you if you are to move beyond the stranglehold of guilt and whatever shame you have felt so burdened by. The rigidity of principles must now make way for sensitivities and your heart will show you the way.

Know this and become aware ...

The more attuned you are to the inner-knowing of your heart's wisdom, the more you will grow in consciousness. Then, when you look back you will see when you were behaving in an unconscious way. You will have more understanding of why your mind left you thinking that guilt was your only option. Without putting yourself through any further suffering, your heart - unburdened by the shackles of rigid principles - will more sensitively enable you to ask, "How can I forgive myself?"

Neither guilt, nor heavily burdened conscience, nor self-recrimination, nor eternal punishment is being demanded of you by Life itself. Only the man-made, mind-made notion of this world and the experience of your Life in it, have insisted you find it such an on-going hardship. Life has no agenda. Life does not judge. The fact that every human being on the planet wakes up to another new day, regardless of whatever 'wrongs' we may believe to be so unforgivable, is testimony to that truth. No matter what perceived 'wrongs' you may have been adjudged to have committed or which you may intentionally have carried out, Life moves you on from the level of unconsciousness you were once at. It opens up to you a new experience, a new chapter, and to a newly informed consciousness. Life is always moving everything on. Realise this important truth.

Know this and become aware ...

The suffering you feel, as a result of guilt, is caused by deriving your sense of self from an unconscious behaviour of the past which you are still carrying into the present. Who You Are now as you are reading this book today, is not the same unconscious 'I' that was operating before today. You are already more enlightened, already more consciously expanded. Move with confidence into that new understanding.

That teaching is as applicable to the monk who is reading this from their monastic cell, as it is to the inmate who is reading it from behind the bars of their prison cell. Life does not judge. It has no agenda. It does not understand the language of reward or punishment. Make sure you do not misjudge Life! Make the decision right now to override past teachings and erroneous beliefs ... become the 'friend' to the universe you once thought you needed to be so 'hostile' towards and which you've been taught to be so much on your guard against. The more in tune you are with your heart, the more elevated will be your communications, actions, and decision making. You will more naturally reach for the higher value, the higher choice.

If we were all more naturally used to consulting the inner-knowing of the heart we would greatly increase our personal responsibility and our society would undergo tremendous change. Co-dependent and manipulative relationships would all but disappear. Trial lawyers would have to find new professions; politicians would be held accountable; people of different faiths would be more tolerant of each other; humanity would act more from love than fear... Life is inviting you to undergo a similar transformation.

Your heart's inner-knowing is not a faculty that can be easily described, in the intellectual sense. It can, however, be experienced. There is no subtleness about the immense energy of the heart. The brain's power pales by comparison. The heart is the largest generator of electromagnetic energy in our body and produces, sends, and receives a broad spectrum of other types and frequencies of energy occurring over time. Wisdom comes from the heart, it is not of the intellect. Because of the heart's central location in our body and the extensive connection it has to all of the cells within our body, its energy transmission becomes highly influential for our body and all of the bodies around us. The heart is constantly pumping energy and information to, from, and within every cell in our body.

Wisdom comes from the innermost depth of your Being, it is not of the head. Follow it, trust it, and move with it. Using your heart intelligence you can compassionately re-tune your awareness towards how you use your personal energy. It can help you reverse exhausting behaviours; starting with *guilt* and then *shame* and then *remorse* and then *regret*, until you come back into alignment with your Source.

This is how to begin communication with your heart. You do so, by building a state of coherence (harmony of heart, spirit, mind and will) ...

Get comfortable and become aware of your breathing. Imagine you are breathing in through your heart area. Breathe a little slower and deeper than usual. When you are in a coherent state, your thoughts and emotions are balanced and you experience ease and inner harmony. In order to still the mind and gain direct access to your heart's intelligence, invite its wisdom to come forth and ask,

"What thoughts, inner-talk and attitudes could
I let go of and which ones help me?"

The more anchored in your heart-centre you are, the less likely you will cave in to old insecurities; guilt, shame, projected fears of the future, worries about the past, self-judgments and doubts. The energetic heart will unfold all the guidance you need ...

Be Patient ... Begin to love the experience of synergy ... Be connected ... Be sensitive to the heart's way... Be united rather than in control ... Be open to subtle energy surprises ... Be confident ... Be gentle ...

To connect with the heart, you have to be more like the heart, allowing a silent but intense presence to dissolve the unconscious patterns of the ego/mind. The memory recall of guilt and its associated thoughts, beliefs, and impulsive reactions, will still remain active for a while—they won't, however, run your Life anymore. The more attuned you become to the inner-knowing of the heart's wisdom, you will realise that you have your own spiritual recording chamber vibrating in the centre of your Being. Every beat of your heart shapes the infinite echoes of your Soul that will resonate long after your body has ceased to serve your Soul's needs.

Close this book now, sit back, become very quiet, ignore your mind's urging to get up and get going and take plenty of time to sense the subtle code tapping in your heart. You will have the wonderful privilege of being a participant observer as you move through *guilt* and *shame* to *remorse*. Then from *remorse* to *regret*, and finally from *regret* to *connectivity* once again. Allow yourself to accept the leap in consciousness which Life is now extending to you. There is nothing you need to 'do', simply allow. Feel the shift moving from the heart to every one of the 75 trillion cells of your body. Let the mind accept its new revelation, its new realisation, its metanoia.

The past was just a lesson, not a Life sentence!

REVELATION. *Easy as it is to do so, it's important not to confuse guilt with morality, as if guilt were some high ideal you are meant to strive to achieve! All moralities are not moral ... Something moral in one country is not in another country. Something moral today was not moral yesterday. Morals change, they are arbitrary. But consciousness is eternal, it never changes. Consciousness is absolute truth.*

REALISATION. *It takes commitment to master living fully in the present moment. This is because present moment awareness is not a state of consciousness that can be attained by the mind's intellect alone. Instead, holding your consciousness in present time is the equivalent of entering a different but parallel dimension of reality. (It is to literally step off the battlefield you once believed Life to be and dropping the belief that it needs to present such a "hostile" existence). There is no need to forget the past - you can hardly forget the past - but by being present more fully than in your past, represents where you position your creative power and your primary identity. The consciousness of present time allows you to keep your memories, but they can no longer hold you hostage and no longer drain your energy, which inevitably drains your health.*

METANOIA. *To let go of the past, you must ascend to a higher truth. Your heart's intelligence will show you the way. Life has no agenda. Give up the ego's power play of blame and shame and know that your guilt, for whatever you thought was so unforgivable, has not stopped you existing. Forgiveness simply means to reach a different place of understanding to the one that you were unconscious of in the past. The moment you allow new understanding to enter your consciousness, an intensity of grace brings healing outside the boundaries of time and space, renewing your Life force.*

CHAPTER NINE

Self forgiveness, conscious reconnection

Nothing in Life is to be feared, it is only to be understood. Now is the time to understand more, so that we might fear less.

–Marie Curie

The key to unraveling any delusion, to seeing through anything that separates us, is to uncover its origin; how it all started to form. This book is written to help you come to that understanding. You have been systematically uncovering many new found revelations and realisations about your Self and about Life, so that you could allow the transformative experience of *metanoia* to penetrate your Being and move beyond guilt's stranglehold. The absolution you have yearned to experience but did not believe you could grant yourself the permission to receive, is now yours. Some of you will have been ready to embrace the teaching of this book, simply because of your openness and willingness to do so. Others will have delved into it out of sheer desperation. Finally, you can now bring to an end your long held misery and any deep wounds from the past.

Know this and become aware ...

All delusions begin in the mind. When you are awake, you will not perceive anything as separate or other than itself. The more aware you become, the more unacceptable it will feel to you if you inadvertently slip back into the identity fiction of the ego.

Whenever you do sense guilt arising and begin to feel its pull, don't push it away, but don't believe it either. Let the guilt be there (as it will initially sit in your consciousness) but go at once to the Source and make conscious connectivity with the Divine. Remember ... all that is man-made and mind-made can now be un-made. If you stay in a state where you're not believing in the pull of guilt but also not pushing it out of your system, then a dissolving happens. If you try to push it away, remember that whatever you resist persists. Whatever you try to push away, you're actually energising. Guilt will begin to take up less room space within you and connectivity with the Divine will be felt in all its completeness.

It's also time to change your vocabulary. The word *Guilt*, of course, is to disappear, as is the use of the following terms and all they imply ... *Blame, Deserve, Fair, Fault*. If you cut out those words from your vocabulary, both in your private thoughts and in your communication with others, you will notice almost immediately that it is far more difficult to fall into negative emotional patterns. You will also become more aware how habitual those patterns had become. All great truths are simple. Living in the present moment is accomplished through creating a spiritual practice. You will be able to cultivate that practice - a Life based on truths - by allowing the wisdom of heart intelligence to be your guide. The more you are attuned to heart intelligence, the more natural you will find it is to live in the present. You will also find that the practice of forgiveness is essential. Without forgiveness, you remain anchored in your past, forever in emotional debt.

As a result of events that turned out to be the way they did, the ego will always want to blame, hold others responsible and keep you feeling unworthy. Because of our programming and conditioning we've all become used to looking for 'justice' to be done, and it is so important to release ourselves from this destructive and vengeful way of thinking. No one is 'bad' and 'sinful' by nature. Rather, we have learned to project these characteristics onto the objects we are viewing in this way. Both virtuous actions and non-virtuous actions arise because of the way we view things, and we have the ability to eliminate ignorant views and replace them by making the higher, more conscious choice.

It is imperative to make present your personal sovereignty and to respect the sovereignty of others.Then you will create the conditions that enable you to take control of your actions, rather than being slaves of anger and craving. To completely eliminate the ignorance that causes you to act from guilt, shame, remorse, or even to act regrettably, you need to purify the negative potentialities placed in your mind by all unconscious actions of the past.

MOVING THROUGH GUILT AND SHAME TO REMORSE. While it's possible to feel guilt without shame, we cannot feel shame without guilt. Shame more readily arises and jumps into action when guilt is our backdrop, generally forming a single complex. The more consciously aware you become, however, the less this complex will be triggered into action. You will not immediately be consumed by deep anguish. You will not immediately feel that you are made 'wrong' or 'bad' for what you perceived you did. Rather, the more natural response of remorse will emerge in its place and will be sufficient to begin anew the new growth process from within.

Unlike guilt, remorse brings you to the possibility of new-found revelations and realisations—a vision of the possible, a glimpse of the peaks. It allows for the heart's wisdom to pave the way forward. It is a considerable leap of consciousness from being mired in guilt. With guilt, you *know* deep down that it's all nonsense, but until you gain further enlightenment, you remain bound by its nonsense. In fact you are hostage to it, never feeling you can stop to question its nonsense. Remorse opens up to you the revelation that the guilt you once felt, belonged to a the level of consciousness you were at in the past. It begins the shift away from guilt's stranglehold by making clear to you the realisation that you are no longer bound by guilt in the present. When you feel remorse, there is so much more your heart will enable you to see, so much more your awareness will allow you to discover about your Self than guilt was ever prepared to permit you. You are undergoing a leap in consciousness and you will feel the difference. Remorse will still be uncomfortable and feel more like the experience of grieving, but far less overwhelming than guilt. Remorse provides you with further opportunity to more fully understand. Guilt had simply kept you imprisoned and rendered you feeling powerless, helpless, and hopeless.

MOVING FROM REMORSE TO REGRET. Remorse and Regret are very similar - but also quite distinct. Remorse is a noun it lacks a verb. In English there is no *"I remorse"*. So in a courtroom, when an offence has been committed - *signs of remorse* are looked for, as well as the person stating "I regret". Signs of remorse indicate not only "I regret being caught", but would also suggest I now have the wisdom, hindsight, and it is now in my consciousness, not to continue to choose that unconscious act of mine again. Regret and Remorse are therefore enough to bring about the deeper realisation that there is another option, a higher choice. No longer is it necessary to continue accommodating guilt. Remorse, unlike guilt, accepts the consequences of past actions, but still suggests that the matter may, as yet, remain unfinished; unaddressed, unhealed, unresolved, unforgiven. Significantly, the root of 'remorse' comes from a word in Anglo-French referring to 'bite' ('mordant'). Remorse means that something may still come back to bite you—a very modern expression! While moving through guilt and shame and replacing it with the feeling of remorse, is to make a significantly more elevated shift in consciousness; the move beyond remorse to the place of regret, is the higher choice still. Interestingly enough, the root of the word 'regret' is of Germanic origin, meaning to 'greet'. And so, to RE-GREET conveys the even more profound expression of re-connectivity.

The move from guilt to the sense of re-connectivity we each long to experience, is the relief and deep gratitude of being at one again with the Divine. It is to re-greet the truth that no matter what we felt so guilty about, the act itself and the memory recall of it, can never keep us separated from the Source of Life. Acceptance of this truth is Self

Forgiveness. Freedom. Acceptance of this truth about your own guilt, empowers you to take more responsibility. It enables you to acknowledge any unconscious behaviours of your past and to act with more wisdom in the present. Acceptance of this truth is about understanding yourself, other people and your Life with more awareness. Acceptance of this truth draws on the heart's intelligence, rather than the programming of the ego/mind you never stopped to question or put differently into perspective.

MOVING BEYOND REGRET TO CONSCIOUS CONNECTIVITY. We can't afford to confuse remorse or regret with guilt. They are not the same. Regret is your announcement that you did not demonstrate your highest choice about Who You Truly Are. Guilt is your decision that you're not worthy of doing so ever again. Society and religions teach you of a guilt which requires you to be punished without hope of rehabilitation, yet Life is constantly resourcing us with the experiences we needed to experience, in order to grow and to expand—that's all it is doing! No test, no punishment for 'failure', no Life-time imprisonment, no need for us to be endlessly proving our worth.

Self Forgiveness is precisely to realise and to re-greet our conscious connectivity to the Divine. In truth, it is a bond we can never be disconnected from - but for as long as we are trapped in the illusion of guilt - it will feel like a connectivity we could never again experience; total acceptance, non-judgmental, non-critical, unconditional love.

Know this and become aware ...

The return to conscious connectivity with the Divine is Self Forgiveness. Your key to Self Forgiveness is not to forgive at all, but to *understand*.

Once you begin to understand how guilt has been formed within you, and how you've formed 'your' conscience around it; once you understand how you have been interpreting and perceiving Life through the beliefs you were given to believe, and through the programming you were conditioned to live by; you begin to *understand* EVERYTHING. And you understand it so very differently.

It is easier now for you to see what has been informing the ways of others, what has been animating them and motivating them. It is also easier for you to understand that they, like you, have been trying to make sense of what has often been the nonsense of their own programmed beliefs, thoughts, and behaviours. For you to forgive the ways of others or to wait hopefully to receive the forgiveness of others, actually becomes unnecessary. Simply forgive yourself, for your unconscious limitations of the past. Everything else then becomes crystal clear.

The belief that made it feel like you needed to judge, shame or blame others, ceases to be your programmed reaction. You wake up from the lie you had been living and guilt becomes redundant. This is not to become cavalier about your past or about whatever hurt you may have caused to others, it is to allow regret to elevate you to a higher state of consciousness. This is the choice which liberates you from the pull of a wounded past.

Everything that occurs in Life is ultimately beneficial to Life, even if to our minds it may not appear to be so. If you feel into guilt and then into regret, you'll easily know the difference. You will never give up regretting some of the things you have said, or done, or thought, but you will no longer feel it necessary to keep hurting yourself over it, as you've done with guilt.

Know this and become aware ...

You once believed that what you were doing or thinking was the only way that you could get what you felt you needed. Now you have more clarity. Now you understand differently. Life allows each of us whatever length of time it takes, to reach a higher state of awareness. You have chosen that time to be NOW.

Have you ever wondered why battered wives or husbands still go back to their partners and re-enact the same dramas, or choose another partner and choose a repeat of the same nightmare experiences? Have you ever really asked what keeps addictive patterns of behaviour as a recurring pattern - REPEAT, REPEAT, REPEAT? The common theme in all cases is GUILT. Its mind-set instils lack of self-acceptance, lack of self-worth, lack of self-love and purpose. An attitude that clearly went back a long time and has become a habitual addictive drama.

The unconscious belief of any person repeating that pattern is that they deserved to be punished for not getting Life more 'right' than they did. Such investment in guilt, then creates the magnetic attraction with more of the same, more of the same, more of the same. Addictions are self-violations and guilt keeps that behaviour in place. The more we indulge in it, we find reasons and rationale to try to excuse our behaviour and we most often do so by creating a 'poor me' melodrama and a victim mentality.

There are also many inmates serving long jail sentences for repeatedly offending, but none of them are known to have really turned their Life around *just* because they felt guilty. It's likely too, that guilt alone will never have empowered you to make significant transformational changes in your Life either. In fact it is more likely that your investment in guilt will have been used by the ego to create your own various acts of sly self-indulgence and self-pity.

The great psychologists Jung and Adler are famous for regarding most guilt of this kind, as a rather cheap substitute for legitimate suffering. They saw guilt as little more than an excuse to opt out from the much harder work of real change. You have now reached a different realisation and your "inner engineering" has now begun. You are now ready to bring a halt to guilt's falsity.

Know this and become aware …

**Guilt is merely another form of self-indulgence.
It is a disguised form of egotism.**

Your deliberate and effortful work of accepting Life's invitation to become more consciously awake and aware, ultimately leads to a death of the ego perspective: the death of all you thought you were, before accepting Life's invitation to make the leap in consciousness you've now initiated.

Inevitably, the beliefs and thoughts and behaviours you once never stopped to question and the convictions you once held so strongly, have now become possible for you to view very differently. Even 'your' conscience has been reviewed and elevated; aligning itself with the inner wisdom of heart intelligence.

To ignore your inner-knowing would be to ignore the course of correction that heart intelligence is offering. The inner-knowing of the heart will always tell you when you have veered from living consciously into an expression of unconsciousness. Be careful that it's your true Self you are listening to and not just old programming. When you are more aware, you will find that it becomes difficult to confuse the two. Consciousness involves discerning the difference between a feeling that's arising quite naturally and healthily within you, and what's emotional baggage from past programming. As you gradually become more conscious, you learn to feel differently and to approach Life differently. Heart, spirit, mind and will are all in alignment.

The ego gets into terrible knots, that's why the guilt you have been feeling will not have made any sense at all to someone else. All of the time, your mind has been interpreting what guilt is for you, *just* for you. Your feeling of guilt has been unique to you. It's only of relevance to you. It only threatens to take power from you. And it is all so unnecessary.

HOW TO RE-CONNECT WITH TRUTH WHENEVER THE RESIDUE OF PAST GUILT ARISES. Immediately, take some precious time out and see if you can identify the feeling of guilt that is yours, and yours alone. Then unravel yourself from it.

• Remind yourself, the present self 'is' and the former self 'was', and, in truth, that which 'was' is not identical with that which 'is'. Guilt, shame, (and even remorse and regret) result from equating the present self that 'is' with the former self that 'was' but actually is no more; they are not the same.

• Remind yourself that the past cannot be re-written but it can be decontextualised so as to be a source of constructive learning; revelation and realisation.

• As you do so, see how programming, conditioning and your own interpretation of past actions has resulted in the burdensome feeling that you have been carrying. Remind yourself that past events or decisions can be ameliorated by realising that "they seemed like a good idea at the time"! They are the actions of an unconscious past, not those of a more conscious present.

• See how the ego has fastened on to guilt and claimed it, as if it were its own.

• See how fear has made you feel separated from your Source and separated from others.

• See how embarrassment and shame have made you feel ashamed.

• Remind yourself that past errors are due to limitation and belong to a certain point in the timeline of evolution, not only personally but also collectively. Avoid the temptation to harm yourself further by adopting the hypothetical stance of "I should have known better". Simply acknowledge and accept that what was acceptable in the past is no longer acceptable ... "I see things differently now".

• Take a nice deep breath—inhale as much as you now choose to receive from Life. Life makes no judgment of you. Life readily continues to provide as much as you allow yourself to receive. Life has no agenda, it simply continues to breathe you, as it always has done. As you exhale, feel the illusion of guilt leaving every cell of your body. Unreal it!

• Adopt a mantra that you say to yourself the moment that a guilty memory or feeling arises again. The following phrases are truths that are particularly effective:

"I'm not that person anymore" or, **"My attention belongs in the present"** or, **"I am not here to suffer anymore".**

Choose the appropriate phrase and repeat it without fail, every time you feel even a hint of guilt. In this way, you are not only telling yourself the truth, for you aren't the person anymore who committed a past misdeed, but you are also giving your mind a new and true directive. This will help to wean it off the old wiring that keeps repeating its impulsive reaction, long after guilt is deserved.

No matter how big or small your guilty secret, no matter if your guilt is nagging or crushing, the way to freedom is always the same. Do whatever it takes until you truly *know, allow,* and *accept,* that you have transcended its programming and functioning. Let forgiveness replace condemnation, NOW.

METANOIA: ABSOLUTION TO LAST A LIFETIME. I now release the heavy burden of guilt, which has kept me from enjoying the completeness I long to experience. I honour the character, the sovereignty, the essence of my Being. New revelations have brought new realisations into my awareness and now I understand, what I did not understand in the past.

Whatever I have done, whatever I *think* I've not done enough, whatever I *think* I may have done, whatever I *think* I should have done, or *think* I should not have done, I know that I am not here to suffer anymore. My attention belongs in the present.

Whatever I have said, whatever I *think* I've not said enough, whatever I *think* I may have said, whatever I *think* I should have said, or *think* I should not have said, I know that I am not here to suffer anymore. My attention belongs in the present.

Whatever I have thought, whatever I *think* I've not thought enough, whatever I *think* I may have thought, whatever I *think* I should have thought, or *think* I should not have thought, I know that I am not here to suffer anymore. My attention belongs in the present.

Whatever I have kept secret, whatever I *think* I've not kept secret enough, whatever secret thoughts I may have been thinking, whatever I *think* I should have kept secret, or *think* I should not have kept secret, I know that I am not here to suffer anymore. My attention belongs in the present.

Whatever I have promised, whatever I *think* I've not promised enough, whatever I *think* I may have promised, whatever I *think* I should have promised, or *think* I should not have promised, I know that I am not here to suffer anymore. My attention belongs in the present.

AFTERWORD AND ACKNOWLEDGEMENTS

The page layout and cover for this book has been beautifully designed and artworked by my nephew Thomas Gray. He is a master at his craft. My niece Katie Gray (in between baby feeds, school pick up and drop off times, and a million other tasks) has found time to patiently proof read the text, making any necessary editing or typo adjustments required. I am truly grateful to them both for their generous and loving contributions.

Although a great many people have impacted my Life and brought me to the more enlightened state I now live—some through their loving guidance and example, others through the considerable pain and challenge they presented me with—no one more than my beautiful wife Anne Louise, has so lovingly assisted me to realise my own connectivity to the Divine. No one has accompanied me throughout the ups and downs of this Lifetime so consistently, compassionately, patiently, gently and wisely. No one has been so understanding, honest, perceptible, encouraging, confident and kindly, as she.

Anne Louise has taught me how to soften my heart, so that I may hear the voice of my Soul. She has also taught me how to listen compassionately and without judgment to those I have committed so many years of my Life to. For me, that sometimes meant exchanging the hard and rigid principles of my own programming and conditioning (most, if not all of them, coming through the channels of my Catholic upbringing), for greater sensitivity and awareness. By example, Anne Louise has shown me the importance of being more attuned to the deeper needs of others and to their individual circumstances: those in addiction, depression, fear, shame, high anxiety, pain, and those who in so many different ways and varying degrees of suffering, have struggled with the burden of guilt.

Anne Louise has supported me to write this book from the conviction and with the sincerity and dedication I now present to you. May its teaching bring you deep peace and the affirmation and validation your heart has always desired, but which you did not believe you had the freedom to exercise. My heartfelt wish for you now, as the Individuation of the Divine that you are, is that you wake up from the lie of guilt, which has kept you feeling so diminished, and restore again the true radiance of your Being.

I kiss you with all my heart my wise and eternal twin soul, Anne Louise.

Men are not free when they are just doing what they like.
Men are only free when they are doing what the deepest Self likes.
And there is getting down to the deepest Self. It takes some diving!

D.H. Lawrence

John Flaherty BA (Hons), M.Sc., is an internationally recognised Life guide, author, and a respected leader in the field of addiction recovery. His groundbreaking book Addiction Unplugged : How To Be Free became the first book of its kind to be written from the perspective of conscious awareness and is translated in English, German, Spanish, Polish and Romanian.

Beginning his career as a Catholic Priest, he later worked in the care of those affected by HIV/AIDS and then specialised in the treatment and recovery of those addicted to alcohol and substance use. John has established and managed several innovative community-based services in England, Ireland and Canada and has worked for high profile private organisations providing psychotherapy, spiritual direction and emotional guidance to those in addiction and to their loved ones. He currently provides personal online mentoring services to those who wish to seek his assistance.

John is a popular and inspirational speaker and has appeared in interviews for TV, Radio and Internet Talk Shows. With his wife Anne Louise he facilitates workshops and seminars, sharing timeless wisdom on cultivating a spiritual practice and teaching practical ways to find emotional freedom and deeper self-fulfilment.

John and Anne Louise live in England.

www.beawarebealive.com

Made in the USA
Middletown, DE
27 February 2020

85447456R10075